Berli

dip in

french

1000
everyday words and phrases

Berlitz Publishing

New York   London   Singapore

Contacting the Editors
Every effort has been made to provide accurate information in this publication, but changes are inevitable. The publisher cannot be responsible for any resulting loss, inconvenience or injury. We would appreciate it if readers would call our attention to any errors or outdated information. We also welcome your suggestions, please contact us at:
comments@berlitzpublishing.com

All Rights Reserved
© 2012 APA Publications (UK) Ltd.
Berlitz Trademark Reg. U.S. Patent Office and other countries. Marca Registrada.
Used under license from Berlitz Investment Corporation.

First Printing: March 2012
Printed in China

Publishing Director: Mina Patria
Commissioning Editor: Kate Drynan
Editorial Assistant: Sophie Cooper
Cover Design: Beverley Speight
Interior Design: Beverley Speight
Production Manager: Raj Trivedi
Cover Illustration: © Beverley Speight

Contents

1000
everyday words and phrases

Introduction

dip into **french** is intended to help you learn some of the most important words and phrases used in everyday French. In mastering these 1,000 words or so, you will be able to converse and get by reading in up to 80% of situations common to daily life. This book can be used as a study aid, as a quick-reference guide on the go or as the basis for learning new vocabulary from scratch. Although this is not a grammar book, it does contain tips on sentence structure and other cultural facts, spread evenly throughout the sections to enable you to learn more effectively. Each word and phrase is set into context with a sample sentence so you know when and how to use it, and the simplified phonetics will guide you through any tricky pronunciations.

There are approximately 129 million French speakers worldwide. French is an official language in 30 countries and the United Nations. French is spoken by four million people in Belgium, seven million in Canada, 60.5 million in France and 1.3 million in Switzerland. It is also an official language of 22 African nations.

Key

adj	adjective	**m**	masculine
adv	adverb	**pl**	plural
abbr	abbreviation	**pron**	pronoun
art	article	**n**	noun
conj	conjunction	**prep**	preposition
f	feminine	**v**	verb

Pronunciation

This section is designed to make you familiar with the sounds of French using our simplified phonetic transcription. You'll find the pronunciation of the French letters and sounds explained below, together with their 'imitated' equivalents. This system is used throughout the book; simply read the pronunciation as if it were English, noting any special rules below.

In French, all syllables are pronounced the same, with no extra stress on any particular syllable. The French language contains nasal vowels, which are indicated in the pronunciation by a vowel symbol followed by an *N*. This *N* should not be pronounced strongly, but it is there to show the nasal quality of the previous vowel. A nasal vowel is pronounced simultaneously through the mouth and the nose.

In French, the final consonants of words are not always pronounced. When a word ending in a consonant is followed with a word beginning with a vowel, the two words are often run together. The consonant is therefore pronounced as if it begins the following word.

Example	Pronunciation
comment	*koh·mawN*
Comment allez-vous?	*koh·mawN tah·lay-voo*

Consonants

Letter	Approximate Pronunciation	Symbol	Example	Pronunciation
cc	1. before e, i, like cc in accident	**ks**	**accessible**	*ahk·seh·see·bluh*
	2. elsewhere, like cc in accommodate	**k**	**d'accord**	*dah·kohr*
ch	like sh in shut	**sh**	**chercher**	*shehr·shay*
ç	like s in sit	**s**	**ça**	*sah*

Letter	Approximate Pronunciation	Symbol	Example	Pronunciation
g	1. before e, i, y, like s in pleasure	**zh**	**manger**	*mawN•zhay*
	2. before a, o, u, like g in go	**g**	**garçon**	*gahr•sohN*
h	always silent		**homme**	*ohm*
j	like s in pleasure	**zh**	**jamais**	*zhah•may*
qu	like k in kill	**k**	**qui**	*kee*
r	rolled in the back of the mouth, like gargling	**r**	**rouge**	*roozh*
w	usually like v in voice	**v**	**wagon**	*vah•gohN*

B, c, d, f, k, l, m, n, p, s, t, v, x and z are pronounced as in English.

Vowels

Letter	Approximate Pronunciation	Symbol	Example	Pronunciation
a, à, â	between the a in hat and the a in father	**ah**	**mari**	*mah•ree*
e	sometimes like a in about	**uh**	**je**	*zhuh*
è, ê, e	like e in get	**eh**	**même**	*mehm*
é, ez	like a in late	**ay**	**été**	*ay•tay*
i	like ee in meet	**ee**	**il**	*eel*
o, ô	generally like o in roll	**oh**	**donner**	*doh•nay*
u	like ew in dew	**ew**	**une**	*ewn*

Sounds spelled with two or more letters

Letter	Approximate Pronunciation	Symbol	Example	Pronunciation
ai, ay, aient, ais, ait, aî, ei	like a in late	**ay**	j'ai vais	*zhay* *vay*
ai, ay, aient, ais, ait, aî, ei	like e in get	**eh**	chaîne peine	*shehn* *pehn*
(e)au	similar to o	**oh**	chaud	*shoh*
eu, eû, u	like u in fur but short like a puff of air	**uh**	euro	*uh•roh*
euil, euille	like uh + y	**uhy**	feuille	*fuhy*
ail, aille	like ie in tie	**ie**	taille	*tie*
ille	1. like yu in yucca 2. like eel	**eeyuh** **eel**	famille ville	*fah-meeyuh* *veel*
oi, oy	like w followed by the a in hat	**wah**	moi	*mwah*
ou, oû	like o in move or oo in hoot	**oo**	nouveau	*noo•voh*
ui	approximately like wee in between	**wee**	traduire	*trah•dweer*

Feedback

Help us to make sure this remains the right book for you by submitting your suggestions to:

comments@berlitzpublishing.com

Alternatively, please write to:

**Berlitz Publishing,
APA Publications Ltd.,
58 Borough High Street,
London SE1 1XF,
United Kingdom**

Distribution

Worldwide
APA Publications GmbH & Co. Verlag KG
(Singapore branch)
7030 Ang Mo Kio Ave 5
08-65 Northstar @ AMK, Singapore 569880
Email: apasin@singnet.com.sg

UK and Ireland
Dorling Kindersley Ltd
(a Penguin Company)
80 Strand, London, WC2R 0RL, UK
Email: sales@uk.dk.com

US
Ingram Publisher Services
One Ingram Blvd, PO Box 3006
La Vergne, TN 37086-1986
Email: customer.service@ingrampublisher
services.com

Australia
Universal Publishers
PO Box 307
St. Leonards NSW 1590
Email: sales@universalpublishers.com.au

Life

People

address *n*
I can give you my **address**.

l'adresse [lah•drehs] *n*
Je peux te donner mon **adresse**.

angry *adj*

en colère, fâché, e
[awN koh•lehr, fah•shay, fah•shay]
loc/adj

My boss is **angry** because
I didn't do the work.

Mon patron est **fâché** parce que je
n'ai pas fait mon travail.

anyone *pron*

quelqu'un; n'importe qui
[kehl•kuhN; nehN•pohr•tuh•kee]
pron/loc

Do you know **anybody** in
Canada?
Bring **anyone** else you like.

Tu connais **quelqu'un** au Canada?

Amenez **n'importe qui** d'autre.

bad *adj*	**mauvais, e** [moh·veh, moh·vehz] *adj*
He isn't a **bad** person!	Ce n'est pas un **mauvais** garçon!
to be *v*	**être** [eh·truh] *v*
Please **be** here tomorrow.	Je vous prie **d'être** là demain.

Fact

You will hear the verb **être** used with a limited number of verbs to form the past tense. These often tend to be verbs of motion, like **sortir, arriver, entrer, tomber, partir**, etc. For example: **Je suis venu voir ma sœur** – I have come to see my sister.

boy *n*	**le garçon** [luh gahr·sohN] *n*
I saw some **boys** running away.	J'ai vu des **garçons** partir en courant.
first name *n*	**le prénom** [luh pray·nohN] *n*
My **first name** is Scottish.	Mon **prénom** est d'origine écossaise.
gentleman *n m*	**le monsieur** [luh muh·see·yuh] *n*
Who is this **gentleman**?	Qui est ce **monsieur?**
girl *n*	**la fille** [lah feeyuh] *n*
There are a lot of **girls**. in the class	Il y a beaucoup de **filles** dans la classe.

happy adj	**content, e; heureux, euse**
	[cohN•tawN, cohN•taWn•tuh;
	uh•ruh] adj
She's very **happy** about	Elle est très **contente** de son
her new job.	nouveau travail.
I've had a **happy** life.	J'ai eu une vie **heureuse**.

| **he** pron m sg | **il** [eel] pron |
| **He** teaches in my school. | **Il** enseigne dans mon école. |

her pron f sg	**lui, l'; son, sa, ses**
	[lwee, l'; sohN, sah, seh] pron
I gave **her** a kiss.	Je **lui** ai donné un baiser.
He saw **her** at the station.	Il **l'**a vue à la gare.
She showed me **her** new books.	Elle m'a montré **ses** nouveaux livres.

him pron m sg	**lui, l'** [lwee, l'] pron
Sure, I gave **him** the book.	Oui, je **lui** ai donné le livre.
I saw **him** last night in the park.	Je **l'**ai vu hier soir dans le parc.

| **his** pron m sg | **son, sa, ses** [sohN, sah, seh] pron |
| He lent me **his** new coat. | Il m'a prêté **son** nouveau manteau. |

Fact

The form **son** is also used for feminine nouns if they begin with a vowel (a,e,i,o,u) or a silent h.

| **I** pron sg | **Je** [zhuh] pron |
| Hi, **I**'m Maggie. | Bonjour, **je** m'appelle Maggie. |

identity card n

*The police wanted to see everybody's **identity cards**.*

la carte d'identité
[lah kahrt dee•dawN•tee•tay] n
*La police a voulu voir les cartes **d'identité** de tout le monde.*

lady n
*There's a **lady** on the phone for you.*

la dame [lah dahm] n
*Il y une **dame** au téléphone pour vous.*

last name n

*Do you know her **last name**?*

le nom de famille
[luh nohN duh fah•meeyuh] n
*Connais-tu son **nom de famille**?*

man (pl men) n
*There was a young **man** in the car.*

l'homme [lohm] n
*Il y avait un jeune **homme** dans la voiture.*

me pron sg
*Don't you see **me**?*
*Why didn't you help **me**?*
*Who's there? – It's **me**.*

me, m', moi [muh, m', mwah] pron
*Tu ne **me** vois pas?*
*Pourquoi tu ne **m'**as pas aidé?*
*Qui est là? – C'est **moi**.*

Fact

Before a vowel (a,e,i,o,u) or a silent h the short form **m'** is used instead of **me**.

Mr n m Brit.
Mr. n m Am.
*Could I speak to **Mr** Tanaka, please?*

M. [muh•see•yuh] n

*Pourrais-je parler à **M.** Tanaka, s'il vous plaît?*

Fact

The correct form of address for adult males is **monsieur**. The plural is **messieurs**. The abbreviated forms are **M.** and **MM.** respectively.

Mrs n f Brit.	*Mme* [mah•dam] n
Mrs. n f Am.	
This is **Mrs** Hank's office.	*Voici le bureau de* **Mme** *Hank.*

Fact

The correct form of address for adult females is **madame**. The plural is **mesdames**. You will regularly see the abbreviated forms **Mme** and **Mmes** on written correspondence.

Ms n f Brit.	**Mme** [ma•duh•mwa•zell] n
Ms. n f Am.	
Please wait outside, **Ms** Green.	*Veuillez attendre dehors,* **Mme** *Green.*

Fact

Young women are addressed as **mademoiselle** (miss). The plural is **Mesdemoiselles**. The abbreviated forms are **Mlle** und **Mlles** respectively are you will see these regularly on written correspondence.

| **my** *pron* | **mon, ma, mes** [mohN, mah, meh] *pron* |
| *Here are **my** jeans.* | *C'est **mon** jean.* |

name *n*	**le nom** [luh nohN] *n*
*That's my **name** there on the letter.*	*C'est mon **nom** qui est inscrit sur cette enveloppe.*
our *pron pl*	**notre; nos** [noh·truh; noh] *pron*
*Look, that's **our** new car.*	*Regarde, c'est **notre** nouvelle voiture.*
passport *n*	**le passeport** [luh pass·pohr] *n*
*I need a new **passport**.*	*J'ai besoin d'un nouveau **passeport**.*
person *n*	**la personne** [lah pehr·sonn] *n*
*I like him as a **person**, but not as a teacher.*	*Je l'apprécie en tant que **personne**, mais pas en tant que professeur.*
she *pron f sg*	**elle** [ell] *pron*
*This is my sister. **She** lives in Canada.*	*Voici ma sœur. **Elle** vit au Canada.*
somebody, someone *pron sg*	**quelqu'un** [kehl·kuhN] *pron*
*Last night **somebody** put this empty bottle on the table.*	*Hier soir, **quelqu'un** a mis cette bouteille vide sur la table.*

that *conj*
The truth is **that** I never loved her.

que [kuh] *conj*
La vérité, c'est **que** je ne l'ai jamais aimée.

---

their *pron pl*
Look, there are Mary and Sally. **Their** father lives in Switzerland.

leur, leurs [luhr, luhr] *pron*
Regarde, voilà Mary et Sally. **Leur** père vit en Suisse.

---

them *pron pl*

Your parents were here and I gave **them** your new book.
Have you seen my new shoes? I can't find **them**.
I'm not talking to **them**.

leur; les; eux, elles
[luhr; leh; uh, el] *pron*
Tes parents étaient là et je **leur** ai offert ton nouveau livre.
As-tu vu mes chaussures? Je ne **les** trouve pas.
Ce n'est pas à **eux** ou **elles** que je parle.

---

they *pron pl*
He gave me some flowers for my birthday. Aren't **they** beautiful?

They say so.

ils, elles [eel, ell] *pron*
Il m'a offert des fleurs pour mon anniversaire. N'est-ce pas qu'**elles** sont belles?
C'est ce qu'**ils** disent.

---

us *pron pl*
He gave **us** a dictionary as a Christmas present.
She saw **us** at the party.

Nous [noo] *pron*
Il **nous** a offert un dictionnaire à Noël.
Elle **nous** a vus à la fête.

---

woman *n*
Eve is a **woman**, Adam is a man.

la femme [lah fahm] *n*
Ève est une **femme**; Adam est un homme.

you *pron sg*

Do **you** speak Spanish?
I'm sure I gave it to **you**.
I saw **you** yesterday.
I'm not talking to **you**.

tu; te, t'; toi
[tew; tuh, t'; twah] *pron*

Est-ce que **tu** parles espagnol?
Je suis certain de **te** l'avoir donné.
Je **t'**ai vu hier.
Ce n'est pas à **toi** que je parle.

Fact

Before a vowel (a,e,i,o,u) or a silent h the short form **t'** is used instead of **te**.

you *pron sg*
Yes, I gave it to **you** a week ago.

Do **you** speak German?

vous (polite form) [voo] *pron*
Oui, je **vous** l'ai donné il y a une semaine.
Parlez-**vous** allemand?

you *pron pl*
Do **you** speak English?
I saw **you** both in the supermarket.
No, I met **you** and I gave it to you.

vous (collective) [voo] *pron*
Parlez-**vous** anglais?
Je **vous** ai vus tous les deux au supermarché.
Non, je vous ai vus et je **vous** l'ai donné.

your *pron sg, pl*
Is this **your** case?

votre; vos [voh•truh; voh] *pron*
Est-ce que c'est **votre** valise?

we *pron pl*
We went outside.

Nous [noo] *pron*
Nous sommes sortis.

Family

boyfriend n

She has got a new **boyfriend**.

le petit ami
[luh puh•tee•tah•mee] n
Elle a un nouveau **petit ami**.

brother n
I often use my **brother's** car.

le frère [luh frehr] n
J'emprunte souvent la voiture
de mon **frère**.

child n
This **child** is very intelligent.
They have got three **children**:
two boys and one girl.

l'enfant [lawN•fawN] n
Cet **enfant** est très intelligent.
Ils ont trois **enfants** : deux garçons
et une fille.

daughter n
My **daughter** is five years old.

la fille [lah feeyuh] n
Ma **fille** a cinq ans.

family n
He brought photographs of
his **family** with him.

la famille [lah fah•meeyuh] n
Il a apporté des photos de
sa **famille**.

father n
Our new teacher is a **father**
of four children.

le père [luh pehr] n
Notre nouveau professeur est **père**
de quatre enfants.

friend n
So, how old is your **friend**?

l'ami, e [lah•mee, lah•mee] n
Alors, quel âge a ton **ami?**

girlfriend n

My son has a different
girlfriend every week.

la petite amie
[lah puh•teet•ah•mee] n
Mon fils a une nouvelle **petite** amie
toutes les semaines.

grandparents n pl

les grands-parents
[leh grawN•pah•rawN] n

John lives with his **grandparents**.	John vit chez ses **grands-parents**.
husband n She wants to come over with her **husband**.	**le mari** [luh mah•ree] n Elle veut venir avec son **mari**.
to meet v Do you want **to meet** my friends? I **met** him in High School.	**rencontrer, faire la connaissance de** [rawN•kohN•tray, fehr•koh•nay•sawN•suh duh] v As-tu envie de **rencontrer** mes amis? J'ai fait sa **connaissance** au lycée.
mother n Her **mother** lives in Paris.	**la mère** [lah mehr] n Sa **mère** vit à Paris.
parents n pl You can't choose your **parents**.	**les parents** [leh pah•rawN] n On ne choisit pas ses **parents**.
to remember v Do you **remember** auntie Helen? – No, I don't **remember** her. Please **remember** to call Ann.	**se souvenir de, se rappeler (de); penser à** [suh soo•vuh•neer duh, suh rah•puh•lay (duh); pawN•say ah] v Tu **te souviens** de tante Helen? – Non, je ne m'en **rappelle** pas. **Pense** à appeler Ann, s'il te plaît.
sister n Yesterday my **sister** arrived back from her holidays in Spain.	**la sœur** [lah suhr] n Ma **sœur** est rentrée hier de ses vacances en Espagne.
son n I hope my **son** chooses a better job.	**le fils** [luh feess] m J'espère que mon **fils** choisira un meilleur métier.

still *adv*	**toujours, encore** [too•zhoor, awN•kohr] *adv*
*Do you **still** like her friend?*	*Tu aimes **toujours** son ami?*
wife *(pl wives)* *n*	**la femme** [lah fahm] *n*
*Have you met my **wife**?*	*Connaissez-vous ma **femme**?*
with *prep*	**avec** [ah•vehk] *prep*
*Mary went to Brighton **with** her father.*	*Mary est allée à Brighton **avec** son père.*

Countries & Languages

Australia *n*	**l'Australie** [loh•strah•lee] *n*
*Sydney is the biggest city in **Australia**.*	*Sydney est la plus grande ville d'**Australie**.*
Australian *adj*	**australien, enne** [oh•strah•lee•yehN, oh•strah•lee•yenn] *adj*
*Do you like **Australian** wine?*	*Aimez-vous le vin **australien**?*
an Australian *n*	**un Australien, une Australienne** [uhN noh•strah•lee•yehN, ewn oh•strah•lee•yenn] *n*
the Australians *n pl*	**les Australiens** [lay zoh•strah•lee•yehN] n
Austria *n*	**l'Autriche** [loh•treesh] *n*
***Austria** is south of Germany.*	***L'Autriche** se trouve au sud de l'Allemagne.*
Austrian *adj*	**autrichien, enne** [oh•tree•shee•yehN, oh•tree•shee•yenn] *adj*

I like **Austrian** music.	J'aime la musique **autrichienne**.
an Austrian n	**un Autrichien,** **une Autrichienne** [uhN noh•tree•shee•yehN, ew noh•tree•shee•yenn] n
the Austrians n pl	**les Autrichiens** n
Great Britain n	**la Grande-Bretagne** [lah grawN•duh bruh•tah•nee•yuh] n
She's from **Great Britain**.	Elle est originaire de **Grande-Bretagne**.
British adj	**Britannique** [bree•tah•neek] adj
She's a **British** citizen.	Elle a la citoyenneté **britannique**.
A Briton n	**un, une Britannique** [uhN bree•tah•neek, ewn bree•tah•neek] n
the British n pl	**les Britanniques** [leh bree•tah•neek] n
Canada n	**le Canada** [luh kah•nah•dah] n
Canada is a very big country.	**Le Canada** est un très grand pays.
Canadian adj	**canadien, enne** [kah•nah•dee•yehN, kah•nah•dee•yenn] adj
Canadian cities are very clean.	Les villes **canadiennes** sont très propres.
a Canadian n	**un Canadien, une Canadienne** [uhN kah•nah•dee•yehN, ewn kah•nah•dee•yenn] n
the Canadians n pl	**les Canadiens** [leh kah•nah•dee•yehN] n

22

country *n*	**le pays** [luh pay·yee] *n*
Cambridge is in the east of the **country**.	Cambridge se situe dans l'est du **pays**.
dictionary *n*	**le dictionnaire** [luh deek·see·oh·nehr] *n*
I didn't find the **dictionary**.	Je n'ai pas trouvé **le dictionnaire**.
England *n*	**l'Angleterre** [lawN·gluh·tehr] *n*
England is south of Scotland.	**L'Angleterre** se trouve au sud de l'Ecosse.
English *adj*	**anglais, e** [awN·gleh, awN·glehz] *adj*
They speak **English**.	Ils parlent **anglais**.
an **Englishman** *(pl -men) n*	**un Anglais** [uhN nawN·gleh] *n*
an **Englishwoman** *(pl -women) n*	**une Anglaise** [ewn awN·glehz] *n*
This **Englishwoman** is quiet.	Cette **Anglaise** est discrète.
the **English** *n*	**les Anglais** *n*
The **English** are a European nation.	**Les Anglais** sont une nation européenne.
English *n*	**l'anglais** [lawN·gleh] *n*
Do you speak **English**?	Parlez-vous **anglais**?
Europe *n*	**l'Europe** [luh·rop] *n*
Europe is much smaller than Africa.	**L'Europe** est beaucoup plus petite que l'Afrique.
European *adj*	**européen, enne** [uh·roh·pay·ehN, uh·roh·pay·ehn] *adj*
There are a lot of **European** languages.	Il existe beaucoup de langues **européennes**.

| a European *n* | **un Européen, une Européenne** [unH nuh•roh•pay•ehN, ewn uh•roh•pay•ehn] *n* |
| the Europeans *n pl* | **les Européens** [lay zuh•roh•pay•ayn] *n* |

everywhere *adv* **partout** [pahr•too] *adv*
Almost **everywhere** in the world people speak English. Presque **partout** dans le monde, on parle anglais.

first language *n* **la langue maternelle** [lah lawNg mah•tehr•nell] *n*
Welsh is my **first language**. Ma **langue maternelle** est le gallois.

foreigner *n* **l'étranger, l'étrangère** [lay•trawN•zhay, lay•trawN•zhehr] *n*
Everyone is a **foreigner** somewhere. Tout le monde est un **étranger** quelque part.

France *n* **la France** [lah frawNs] *n*
He met her on his first trip to **France**. Il l'a rencontrée lors de son premier voyage en **France**.
French *adj* **français, e** [frawN•seh, frawN•sehz] *adj*
We tasted wonderful **French** wines. Nous avons goûté d'extraordinaires vins **français**.
French *n* **le français** [luh frawN•seh] *n*
Do you speak **French**? Parlez-vous **français?**
a Frenchman *(pl -men) n* **un Français** [uhN frawN•seh] *n*
a Frenchwoman *(pl -women)* **une Française** [uhn frawN•sehz] n
He is married to a **Frenchwoman**. Il est marié à une **Française**.

the French *n pl*
There are plenty of stereotypes about the **French**.

les Français [lay frawN•seh] *n*
Beaucoup de stéréotypes circulent sur le compte des **Français**.

Germany *n*

l'Allemagne [lah•luh•mah•nee•yuh] *n*

He is in **Germany**.
German *adj*

Il est en **Allemagne**.
allemand, e [ah•luh•mawN, ah•luh•mawNd] *adj*

I bought some **German** books.

J'ai acheté quelques livres **allemands**.

German *n*
Do you speak **German**?
a **German** *n*

l'allemand [lah•luh•mawN] *n*
Parlez-vous **allemand?**
un Allemand, une Allemande [uhN nah•luh•mawN, ewn ah•luh•mawNd] *n*

the German *n pl*

les Allemands [lay zah•luh•mawN] *n*

international *adj*

international, e [ehN•ter•nah•see•o•nahl, ehN•ter•nah•see•o•nahl] *adj*

The **international** airport is close to the city.

L'aéroport **international** est proche de la ville.

Ireland *n*
Ireland is a country to the west of England.
Irish *adj*

l'Irlande [leer•lawNd] *n*
L'Irlande est un pays situé à l'ouest de l'Angleterre.
irlandais, e [eer•lawN•deh, eer•lawN•dehz] *adj*

I like **Irish** pubs.

J'aime les pubs **irlandais**.

an Irishman (pl -men) (-men) n   **un Irlandais**
[unH neer·lawN·deh] n

an Irishwoman (pl -women) n   **une Irlandaise**
[ewn eer·lawN·dehz] n

*We met a lot of **Irishmen** in*   *Nous avons rencontré beaucoup*
*the pub but no **Irishwomen**.*   *d'Irlandais au pub, mais pas*
d'Irlandaises.

the Irish n pl   **les Irlandais** [lay· zeer·lawN·deh] n
*The **Irish** are descendants of*   ***Les Irlandais** descendent*
Viking invaders.   *d'envahisseurs viking.*

Italy n   **l'Italie** [lee·tah·lee] n
*He loves **Italy**.*   *Il adore l'Italie.*
Italian adj   **italien, enne** [ee·tah·lee·ehN] adj
*I love **Italian** food.*   *J'adore la cuisine **italienne**.*
Italian n   **l'italien** [lee·tah·lee·ehN] n
*Do you speak **Italian**?*   *Parlez-vous **italien**?*
an Italian n   **un Italien, une Italienne**
[uhN nee·tah·lee·ehN, ewn
ee·tah·lee·yenn] n

*He's an **Italian**.*   *C'est un **Italien**.*
the Italians n pl   **les Italiens** [leh zee·tah·lee·ehN] n

language n   **la langue** [lah lawNg] n
*How many **languages** do*   *Combien de **langues** parlez-vous?*
you speak?

to live v   **vivre** [vee·vruh] v
*My father's brother **lives** in*   *Mon oncle **vit** en Afrique centrale.*
Central Africa.

nation n
The whole **nation** listened to the speech on the radio.

la nation [lah nah•see•ohN] n
La nation tout entière a écouté le discours à la radio.

national adj

The French **national** holiday is celebrated on 14 July each year.

national, e [nah•see•o•nahl, nah•see•o•nahl] adj
En France, la fête **nationale** est célébrée chaque année le 14 juillet.

nationality n

What **nationality** is he?

la nationalité [lah nah •see•o•na•lee•tay] n
Quelle est sa **nationalité**?

never adv
It's **never** too late to learn a new language.

jamais [zha•meh] adv
Il n'est **jamais** trop tard pour apprendre une nouvelle langue.

people n pl
In many countries **people** don't eat pork.

les gens [lay zhawN] n
Dans beaucoup de pays, **les gens** ne mangent pas de porc.

Spain n
He's bought a house in **Spain**.

l'Espagne [less•pah•nyuh] n
Il a acheté une maison en **Espagne**.

Fact

Feminine countries and regions have **en** for in.

Spanish adj
Spanish n
Do you speak **Spanish**?

espagnol, e [ess•pah•nyol] adj
l'espagnol [less•pah•nee•ol] n
Parlez-vous **espagnol?**

the Spanish n pl

The **Spanish** are known for their warm hospitality.
a Spaniard n

Tina's married to a **Spaniard**.
the Spaniards n pl

les Espagnols
[leh zess•pah•nyol] n

Les Espagnols sont réputés pour leur accueil chaleureux.
un Espagnol, une Espagnole
[uhN ness•pah•nyol, ewn ess•pah•nyol] n
Tina est mariée à **un Espagnol**.
les Espagnols
[leh zess•pah•nyol] n

state n
The U.S. has fifty **states**.

l'Etat [lay•tah] n
Les Etats-Unis d'Amérique comptent cinquante **Etats**.

Switzerland n
Switzerland is a small country with high mountains.
Swiss adj
Do you often eat **Swiss** cheese?

a Swiss n

the Swiss n pl

la Suisse [lah sweess] n
La Suisse est un petit pays de hautes montagnes.
Suisse [sweess] adj
Mangez-vous souvent du fromage **suisse**?
un Suisse, une Suisse/ une Suissesse [uhN sweess, ewn sweess/ewn sweess•ess] n
les Suisses [leh sweess] n

too adv
I can speak Spanish **too**.
You're speaking **too** fast, I don't understand!

aussi; trop [oh•see; troh] adv
Je parle **aussi** espagnol.
Tu parles **trop** vite, je ne comprends pas!

United States of America *n*	**les Etats-Unis d'Amérique** [leh•zay•tah•zew•nee•dah may•ree k] *n*
Jackie comes from the **United States**.	*Jackie vient des **Etats-Unis**.*
America *n*	**l'Amérique** [lah•may•reek] *n*
My brother lives in South **America**.	*Mon frère vit en **Amérique** du Sud.*
American *adj*	**américain, e** [ah•may•ree•kehN, ah•may•ree•kehn] *adj*
New York is an **American** city.	*New York est une ville **américaine**.*
an American *n*	**un Américain, une Américaine** [uhN nah•may•ree•kehN, Américain, ew nah•may•ree•kay•nuh] *n*
the Americans *n pl*	**les Américains** [lay zah•may•ree•kehN] *n*

Nature & Animals

animal *n*	**l'animal** [lah•nee•mal] *n*
He likes all kinds of **animals**.	*Il aime toutes sortes d'**animaux**.*
bird *n*	**l'oiseau** [lwah•zoh] *n*
I could hear the **birds** in the trees.	*J'entendais les **oiseaux** chanter dans les arbres.*
cat *n*	**le chat** [luh shah] *n*
Do you like **cats**?	*Aimez-vous les **chats**?*

chicken
Chickens lay eggs.

la poule [lah poohl] *n*
*Les **poules** pondent des œufs.*

countryside *n*

Do you like living in the
countryside?

la campagne
[lah kawN•pah•nyuh] *n*
*Vous aimez vivre à la
campagne?*

cow *n*
My parents have a small farm
in Wales with a few **cows**
and sheep.

la vache [lah vash] *n*
*Mes parents ont une petite ferme
au pays de Galles avec quelques
vaches et des moutons.*

dog *n*
My **dog** is my best friend.

le chien [luh shee•ehN] *n*
*Mon **chien** est mon meilleur ami.*

fish *n*
There are lots of **fish** in this river.

le poisson [luh pwah•sohN] *n*
*Il y a beaucoup de **poissons** dans
cette rivière.*

flower *n*
You have beautiful **flowers**
in your garden.

la fleur [lah fluhr] *n*
*Vous avez des **fleurs** magnifiques
dans votre jardin.*

fly *n*
There are lots of **flies** in the
house in the country.

la mouche [lah moosh] *n*
*Il y a beaucoup de **mouches** dans
la maison de campagne.*

to follow *v*
All the dogs are **following** me.

suivre [swee•vruh] *v*
*Tous les chiens me **suivent**.*

forest *n*
Shall we go for a walk in
the **forest**?

la forêt [lah foh•reh] *n*
*Et si on allait se promener en **forêt**?*

goat *n* My mother likes **goat's** milk very much.	**la chèvre** [lah sheh•vruh] *n* Me mere aime beaucoup le lait de **chèvre**.
grass *n* I want to lie down on the **grass**. Don't walk on the **grass**.	**l'herbe, le gazon, la pelouse** [lehrb, luh gah•zhohN, lah puh•looz] *n* J'ai envie de m'allonger dans **l'herbe**. **Pelouse** interdite.
to hear *v* Can you **hear** a dog barking?	**entendre** [awN•tawN•druh] *v* Est-ce que tu **entends** un chien aboyer?
horse *n* Have you ever ridden a **horse**?	**le cheval** [luh shuh•val] *n* Es-tu déjà monté à **cheval**?
leaf *n* Many trees lose their **leaves** in autumn.	**la feuille** [lah fuh•yuh] *n* En automne, beaucoup d'arbres perdent leurs **feuilles**.
mouse *n* This **mouse** is white.	**la souris** [lah soo•ree] *n* Cette **souris** est blanche.
pig *n* On the farm we saw cows and **pigs**.	**le cochon** [luh coh•shohn] *n* On a vu des vaches et des **cochons** à la ferme.
plant *n* The **plant** needs more water.	**la plante** [lah plawNt] *n* **La plante** a besoin plus d'eau.
rabbit *n* Christine has two **rabbits** in the garden.	**le lapin** [luh lah•pehN] *n* Christine a deux **lapins** dans le jardin.

rose *n*	**la rose** [lah rohz] *n*
My parents' garden is full of **roses**.	Le jardin de mes parents est plein de **roses**.
sheep *n*	**le mouton** [luh moo•tohN] *n*
We saw lots of **sheep** while driving through Scotland.	Nous avons vu beaucoup de **moutons** en parcourant l'Écosse en voiture.
spider *n*	**l'araignée** [lah•reh•nyay] *n*
I'm scared of **spiders**.	J'ai peur des **araignées**.
tree *n*	**l'arbre** [lahr•bruh] *n*
I like **trees**.	J'aime les **arbres**.

Describing Things

a *art*	**un, une** [uhN, ewn] *art*
an *art*	
That's **a** nice car.	C'est **une** belle voiture.
beautiful *adj*	**beau, belle** [boh, bell] *adj*
What a **beautiful** little boy!	Quel **beau** petit garçon!

Fact

Before masculine nouns beginning with a vowel (a,e,i,o,u) or a silent h, **bel** in the masculine form is used.

| best *adj* | **mieux, le meilleur, la meilleure** [mee•uh, luh meh•yuhr, lah meh•yuhr] *adj* |

It's **best** to buy the tickets now.	Il vaut **mieux** acheter les billets maintenant.
Jackie is the **best** student in my class.	Jackie est **la meilleure** élève de ma classe.
better adj	**mieux** [mee•uh] adj
It's **better** to put the books away today.	Il vaut **mieux** ranger les livres pour aujourd'hui.
big adj	**grand, e** [grawN, grawNd] adj
Cambridge is not really a very **big** town.	Cambridge n'est pas vraiment une très **grande** ville.
black adj	**noir, e** [nwar, nwar] adj
She's got three **black** dresses.	Elle a trois robes **noires**.
blue adj	**bleu, e** [bluh, bluh] adj
Her eyes are very **blue**.	Ses yeux sont très **bleus**.
brown adj	**marron** [mah•rohN] adj
She's got a **brown** coat.	Elle a un manteau **marron**.
centimetre n Brit.	**le centimètre** [luh sawN•tee•meh•truh] n
centimeter n Am.	
My son's now at least two **centimetres** taller than me.	Mon fils mesure maintenant au moins 2 **centimètres** de plus que moi.
colour n Brit.	**la couleur** [la couleur] n
color n Am.	
That's a very nice **colour**.	C'est une très jolie **couleur**.
cool adj fam	**cool** [cool] adj

*She looks **cool** with her new glasses.* — *Elle a l'air **cool** avec ses nouvelles lunettes.*

dark *adj* — **sombre; foncé, e** [sohN•bruh; fohN•say, fohN•say] *adj*

*The night was very **dark**.* — *La nuit était très **sombre**.*
*She's got **dark** hair and blue eyes.* — *Elle a les cheveux **foncés** et les yeux clairs.*

difference *n* — **la différence** [lah dee•fay•rawNs] *n*

*What's the **difference**?* — *Quelle **différence** cela fait-il?*

different *adj* — **différent, e** [dee•fay•rawN, dee•fay•rawNt] *adj*

*These people are very **different**.* — *Ces gens sont très **différents**.*

difficult *adj* — **difficile** [dee•fee•seel] *adj*
*It wasn't **difficult** at first.* — *Au début, ce n'était pas **difficile**.*

dirty *adj* — **sale** [sahl] *adj*
*Take your **dirty** shoes off!* — *Retire ces chaussures **sales**!*

easy *adj* — **facile** [fah•seel] *adj*
*It's very **easy**.* — *C'est très **facile**.*

fair *adj* — **blond, e** [blohN, blohNd] *adj*
*She's got **fair** hair.* — *Elle a les cheveux **blonds**.*

fast *adj* — **rapide** [rah•peed] *adj*
*She's got a **fast** car.* — *Sa voiture est **rapide**.*

to go well *loc* — **bien aller** [bee•yehN•nah•lay] *loc*
*Yeah, the shirt **goes well** with the trousers.* — *Oui, cette chemise **va bien** avec ton pantalon.*

good *adj*	**bon, bonne; sage** [bohN, bonn; sazh] *adj*
She's a very **good** tennis player.	C'est une très **bonne** joueuse de tennis.
I hope the children will be **good** when they visit you.	J'espère que les enfants seront **sages** quand ils viendront chez vous.
great *adj*	**génial, e** [zhay•nee•yahl, zhay•nee•yahl] *adj*
This evening was **great**.	La soirée était **géniale**.
green *adj*	**vert, e** [vehr, vehrt] *adj*
I'll have the **green** apple.	Je prendrai la pomme **verte**.
important *adj*	**important, e** [ehN•pohr•tawN, ehN•pohr•tawNt] *adj*
It is **important** to help her.	Il est **important** de l'aider.
high *adj*	**haut, e** [oh, oht] *adj*
This is a very **high** building.	Cet immeuble est très **haut**.
inch *n*	**le pouce** [luh pooss] *n*
He's two **inches** smaller than me.	Il mesure 2 **pouces** de moins que moi.
interested *adj*	**intéressé, e** [ehN•tay•ray•say, ehN•tay•ray•say] *adj*
We are very **interested** in your plans.	Nous sommes très **intéressés** par votre projet.
interesting *adj*	**intéressant, e** [ehN•tay•ray•sawN, ehN•tay•ray•sawNt] *adj*
There are some **interesting** people here.	Il y a des gens très **intéressants** ici.

kind *adj*	**gentil, ille** [zhawN•tee, zhawN•tee•hy] *adj*
She is very **kind** to old people.	Elle est très **gentille** avec les personnes âgées.
like *prep* It looks **like** gold but it isn't.	**comme** [kohm] *prep* Ça brille **comme** de l'or, mais ça n'en est pas.
to like *v* I **like** hot chocolate.	**aimer** [ay•may] *v* J'**aime** le chocolat chaud.
little *adj* It's a **little** village with six hundred people.	**petit, e** [puh•tee, puh•teet] *adj* C'est un **petit** village de six cents habitants.
to look *v* That **looks** very nice.	**avoir l'air** [ah•vwahr lair] *v* Ça a **l'air** très sympa.
to be lucky *loc* It was **lucky** for him that the police were there.	**avoir de la chance** [ah•vwahr duh lah shawN•suh] *loc* Il a eu **de la chance** que la police soit là.

Fact

If you are wishing somebody good luck, you would say: **bonne chance**, or **bon courage** in French.

new *adj* I want to buy a **new** car.	**nouveau, nouvelle** [noo•voh, noo•vell] *adj* Je veux acheter une **nouvelle** voiture.

nice *adj*
Juliane is very **nice**, isn't she?

sympa [sehN•pah] *adj*
Juliane est très **sympa**, non?

old *adj*
There were all kinds of **old** buildings there.

vieux, vieille
[vee•yuh, vee•ay•yuh] *adj*
Il y avait toutes sortes de **vieux** immeubles là-bas.

Fact

Before masculine nouns beginning with a vowel (a,e,i,o,u) or a silent h, **vieil** in the masculine form is used.

on *prep*
What's that **on** your coat?

sur [sewr] *prep*
Qu'est-ce que t'as **sur** ton manteau?

red *adj*
The traffic light changed to **red**.

rouge [roozh] *adj*
Le feu est passé au **rouge**.

slim *adj*
You look so **slim**!

mince [mehN•suh] *adj*
T'es vraiment **mince!**

slow *adj*
The bus is very **slow** today.

lent, e [lawN, lawNt] *adj*
Le bus est très **lent** aujourd'hui.

small *adj*
She's **small** and has brown hair.

petit, e [puh•tee, puh•teet] *adj*
Elle est **petite** avec des cheveux châtains.

soft *adj*
The bed was too **soft**, I couldn't sleep very well.

mou, molle [moo, moll] *adj*
Le lit était si **mou** que je n'ai pas réussi à dormir.

than *conj*
*You're bigger **than** my brother.*

que [kuh] *conj*
*Tu es plus grand **que** mon frère.*

the *art*
***The** film was not good.*

le, la [luh, lah] *art*
***Le** film était nul.*

Fact

Before a vowel (a,e,i,o,u) or a silent h the short form **l'** is used instead of **le** and **la**.

the *art*
***The** books are fascinating.*

les [leh] *art*
***Les** livres sont fascinants.*

to be unlucky *loc*

**ne pas avoir de chance;
porter malheur**
[nuh pah ah•vwah duh shawN•suh;
por•tay mah•luhr] *loc*

*He's always **unlucky**.
Many people think thirteen is **unlucky** number.*

*Il n'a jamais **de chance**.
Beaucoup de gens croient an que le nombre treize **porte malheur**.*

white *adj*

blanc, blanche
[blawN, blawNsh] *adj*

*I'd like a glass of **white** wine, please.*

*Je voudrais un verre de vin **blanc**, s'il vous plaît.*

worse *adj*
*It's **worse** than I thought.*

pire [peer] *adj*
*C'est **pire** que je ne croyais.*

worst *adj*
*That's the **worst** cake I've ever eaten.*

le pire [luh peer] *adj*
*C'est **le pire** gâteau que j'aie jamais mangé.*

yellow *adj*
This apple is almost **yellow**.

jaune [zhohn] *adj*
Cette pomme est presque **jaune**.

Fact

In French you always place the color after the noun it is describing.
For example: **Une pomme rouge** – a red apple.

young *adj*
She's too **young** to drive a car.

jeune [zhuh•nuh] *adj*
Elle est trop **jeune** pour conduire
une voiture.

The Body

arm *n* He has broken his **arm**.	**bras** [luh brah] *n* Il s'est cassé le **bras**.
back *n* He stood with his **back** to the wall.	**le dos** [luh doh] *n* Il se tenait **le dos** au mur.
to comb *v* Why don't you **comb** your hair?	**se peigner** [suh peh•nyay] *n* Pourquoi tu ne te **peignes** pas?
deodorant *n* Sylvie uses another **deodorant**.	**le déodorant** [luh day•oh•doh•rawN] *n* Slyvie utilise un autre **déodorant**.
ear *n* He hurt his right **ear** in the accident.	**l'oreille** [loh•reh•yuh] *n* Il s'est blessé à **l'oreille** droite dans l'accident.

eye *n*	**l'œil** [luh•yuh] *n*
eyes *pl*	**les yeux** [leh zyuh] *n*
*He closed one **eye**.*	*Il a fermé un **œil**.*
*Susan's got green **eyes**.*	*Susan a **les yeux** verts.*
finger *n*	**le doigt** [luh dwah] *n*
*Thomas has hurt his **finger**.*	*Thomas s'est fait mal au **doigt**.*
foot *n*	**le pied** [luh pee•yay] *n*
*Tom has hurt his left **foot**.*	*Tom s'est fait mal au **pied** gauche.*
hair *n*	**les cheveux** [leh shuh•vuh] *n*
*Mary washed her **hair**.*	*Mary s'est lavé **les cheveux**.*
hairbrush *n*	**la brosse à cheveux** [lah brohs ah shuh•vuh] *n*
*I forgot my **hairbrush**.*	*J'ai oublié ma **brosse**.*
hand *n*	**la main** [lah mehN] *n*
*He cut his **hand**.*	*Il s'est coupé à **la main**.*
head *n*	**la tête** [lah teht] *n*
*She hurt her **head** in the accident.*	*Elle s'est blessée à **la tête** dans l'accident.*
knee *n*	**le genou** [luh zhuh•noo] *n*
*I'm going to have an operation on my **knee**.*	*Je vais me faire opérer **le genou**.*
leg *n*	**la jambe** [lah zhawNb] *n*
*She broke her **leg** last month.*	*Elle s'est cassé **la jambe** le mois dernier.*
mouth *n*	**la bouche** [lah •boosh] *n*
*Open your **mouth**, please.*	*Ouvrez **la bouche**, s'il vous plaît.*

shampoo n	**le shampooing** [luh shawn•poo•ehN] n
I forgot the **shampoo**.	J'ai oublié **le shampooing**.
shoulders n	**les épaules** [lehz eh•pohl] n
He carried his son on his **shoulders**.	Il portait son fils sur ses **épaules**.
shower gel n	**le gel de douche** [luh zhehl duh doosh] n
Do you have **shower gel**?	Avez-vous du **gel de douche**?
skin	**la peau** [lah poh] n
I have sensitive **skin**.	J'ai **la peau** sensible.
stomach n	**l'estomac** [lehss•toh•mah] n
My **stomach** hurts.	J'ai mal à l'estomac.
tissue n	**le mouchoir** [luh moo•shwar] n
Do you have a **tissue**?	Est-ce que tu as un **mouchoir**?
toe n	**l'orteil** [lohr•tey] n
My **toe** hurts.	J'ai mal à **l'orteil**.
toilet roll n	**le papier toilette** [luh pah•pee•yay duh twah•leht] n
We need some **toilet roll**.	On a besoin du **papier toilette**!
tooth n	**la dent** [lah dawN] n
My **tooth** hurts.	J'ai mal à la **dent**.
toothpaste n	**le dentifrice** [luh dawN•tee•frees] n
Do you have **toothpaste**?	Avez-vous du **dentifrice**?

towel n	**la serviette (de bain)** [lah ser•vyehtt (duh behN)] n
*I had to ask reception to bring clean **towels**.*	*J'ai dû réclamer des **serviettes** propres à la réception.*
to wash v	**laver** [lah•vay] v
*Boys, **wash** your hands, please.*	*Les garçons, **lavez**-vous les mains, s'il vous plaît.*

Health & Emergencies

accident n	**l'accident** [lak•see•dawN] n
*He had a bad **accident** last week.*	*Il a eu un grave **accident** la semaine dernière.*
ambulance n	**l'ambulance** [lawN•bew•lawNs] n
*Call for an **ambulance**!*	*Appelez vite une **ambulance**!*
to believe v	**croire** [krwahr] v
*The police didn't **believe** his story.*	*La police n'a pas **cru** son histoire.*
careful adj	**attention** [ah•tawN•see•yohN] adj
*Be **careful**! There's a car coming.*	***Attention**! Une voiture arrive.*
chemist's n Brit. **drugstore** n Am.	**la pharmacie** [lah far•mah•see] n
*Is there a **chemist's** near here?*	*Est-ce qu'il y a une **pharmacie** près d'ici?*
cold n	**le rhume** [luh rewm] n
*I've got a bad **cold**.*	*J'ai attrapé un mauvais **rhume**.*
cough n	**la toux** [lah too] n
*You have quite a bad **cough**.*	*Tu as une mauvaise **toux**.*

| **danger** n | **le danger** [luh dawN·zhay] n |
| No, my life was not in **danger**. | Non, ma vie n'était pas en **danger**. |

| **dentist** n | **le/la dentiste**
[luh/lah dawN·teest] n |
| I went to the **dentist's** yesterday. | Hier, je suis allé chez **le dentiste**. |

| **to die** v | **mourir** [moo·reer] v |
| Seven people **died** in
the accident. | Sept personnes **sont mortes**
dans l'accident. |

| **disabled** adj | **handicapé, e** [awN·dee·kah·pay,
awN·dee·kah·pay] adj |
| Our teacher has got a
disabled daughter. | Notre professeur a une fille
handicapée. |

| **doctor** n | **le médecin** [luh may·duh·sehN] n |
| I went to the **doctor's** yesterday.
I was ill. | Hier, je suis allé chez **le médecin**.
J'étais malade. |

Fact

The masculine form **le medecin** is also used when you are referring
to a female doctor as it is considered a neutral term.

drug n	**le médicament; la drogue** [luh may·dee·kah·mawN; lah drog] n
The doctor prescribed a **drug**.	Le médecin a prescrit un **médicament**.
Drugs are a serious problem in this day and age.	**La drogue** est un grave problème à notre époque.

to find out *v*
The police wants **to find out** everything.

découvrir [day·koo·vreer] *v*
La police cherche à tout **découvrir**.

fire *n*
There was a **fire** in the town center last night.

l'incendie [lehN·sawN·dee] *n m*
Il a y eu un **incendie** dans le centre-ville la nuit dernière.

flu *n*
My husband can't go to work this week. He's got the **flu.**

la grippe [lah greep] *n*
Mon mari ne peut pas aller travailler cette semaine. Il a **la grippe**.

to get better *loc*
He was very ill, but he's **getting better** now.

aller mieux [ah·lay mee·yuh] *loc*
Il a été très malade, mais il va **mieux** maintenant.

have got *v*
I don't feel well, I'**ve got** a cold.

avoir [ah·vwar] *v*
Je ne me sens pas bien, j'**ai** un rhume.

headache *n*

I woke up this morning with a terrible **headache**.

le mal de tête
[luh mahl duh teht] *n*
Je me suis réveillée ce matin avec un terrible **mal de tête**.

healthy *adj*

She's never ill. She is very **healthy**.

en bonne santé
[awN bonn sawN·tay] *loc*
Elle n'est jamais malade. Elle est en très **bonne santé**.

hospital *n*
Jack's mother is in **hospital**.

l'hôpital [loh·pee·tahl] *n*
La mère de Jack est à l'**hôpital**.

to hurt v

*My right ear **hurts**.*
*He **hurt** his leg in the crash.*

faire mal, se blesser
[fehr mahl, suh blay•say] v
*Mon oreille droite me **fait mal**.*
*Il **s'est blessé** à la jambe dans l'accident.*

---

ill adj
*He's **ill** in bed.*

malade [mah•lahd] adj
*Il est **malade** et reste au lit.*

---

medicine n

*Did you take your **medicine** this morning?*

le médicament
[luh may•dee•kah•mawN] n
*As-tu pris ton **médicament** ce matin?*

---

to need v

*I **need** to see a doctor!*

avoir besoin de
[ah•vwar buh•zwehN] loc
*J'ai **besoin** de voir un médecin!*

---

pain n

*I've got a terrible **pain** in my right leg.*

la douleur
[lah doo•luhr] n
*Je ressens une **douleur** terrible dans la jambe droite.*

---

pill n

*Take two **pills** with a glass of water.*
*She's on the **pill**.*

la pilule; la pilule
[lah pee•lewl; lah pee•lewl]
(contraceptive) n
*Vous avalerez deux de ces **pilules** avec un verre d'eau.*
*Elle prend **la pilule**.*

---

police n pl
*The **police** couldn't find the money.*

la police [lah poh•lees] n
*La **police** n'a pas retrouvé l'argent.*

---

sick adj
I felt **sick** on the ferry too.

malade [mah·lahd] adj
Moi aussi j'ai été **malade** sur le ferry.

to smoke v
Please don't **smoke** in this room.

fumer [few·may] v
Prière de ne pas **fumer** dans cette pièce.

waiting room n

la sale d'attente [lah sahl dah·tawNt] n

The **waiting room** is very big.

La sale d'attente est très grande.

Day to Day

At Home

at home *loc*
I think I'll stay at **home** tonight.

à la maison [ah lah may•zohN] *loc*
Je crois que je vais rester
à la maison ce soir.

---

bath *n*

I'd like a room with a **bath**.

I'd like to take a **bath**.

la bagnoire; le bain
[lah bayn•war; luh behN] *n*
J'aimerais une salle de bains avec
baignoire.
J'aimerais prendre un **bain**.

---

bathroom *n*

The house has three **bathrooms**.

la salle de bains
[lah sahl duh behN] *n*
La maison est équipée de trois
salles de bains.

bed *n*
The children go to **bed** at 8:30 p.m.

le lit [luh lee] *n*
Les enfants vont au **lit** à 20h30.

bedroom *n*
This house has four **bedrooms**.

la chambre [lah shawN•bruh] *n*
La maison a quatre **chambres**.

chair *n*
The **chairs** are very comfortable.

la chaise [lah shehz] *n*
Les chaises sont très confortables.

clock *n*

We have a new **clock** in the living room.

l'horloge, la pendule
[lor•lozh, lah pawN•dewl] *n*
Nous avons une nouvelle **horloge** dans le salon.

Come in! *loc*
Come in, please! The door is open.

Entrez! [awN•tray] *v*
Entrez, je vous en prie! C'est ouvert.

comfortable *adj*
This chair is not very **comfortable**.

confortable [kohN•for•ta•bluh] *adj*
Cette chaise n'est pas très **confortable**.

door *n*
The **door** is closed.

la porte [lah port] *n*
La porte est fermée.

electric *adj*
This shop sells **electric** machines.

électrique [ay•lehk•treek] *adj*
Cette boutique vend des appareils **électriques**.

electricity *n*

I forgot to pay the **electricity** bill.

l'électricité
[lay•lehk•tree•see•tay] *n*
J'ai oublié de payer la facture d'**électricité**.

entrance *n*
Please use the front **entrance**.

l'entrée [lawN•tray] *n*
Veuillez emprunter l'**entrée** de devant.

exit n
Where's the **exit** of this building?

la sortie [lah sor•tee] n
Où est **la sortie** de ce bâtiment?

first floor n Brit.

le premier étage
[luh pruhm•yay ay•tazh] n

I don't want to live on the
first floor.

Je ne veux pas vivre au **premier
étage**.

foot n
The table is about six **feet** long.

le pied [luh pee•ay] n
La table mesure environ six **pieds**
de long.

flat n Brit.

l'appartement
[lah•pahr•tuh•mawN] n

apartment n Am.
Is that your **flat**?

Est-ce que c'est votre **appartement**?

floor n
We have rooms on
different **floors**.

l'étage [lay•tazh] n
Nous avons des chambres à
différents **étages**.

fridge n

le réfrigérateur, le Frigidaire®
[luh ray•free•zhee•rah•tuhr, luh
free•zhee•dehr] n

We need a new **fridge**.

Nous avons besoin d'un nouveau
réfrigérateur.

ground floor n Brit.

le rez-de-chaussée
[luh ray duh shoh•say] n

first floor n Am.
We live on the **ground floor**.

Nous vivons au **rez-de-chaussée**.

garage n
On Sundays we normally leave
our car in the **garage**.

le garage [luh gah•rahzh] n
D'ordinaire, le dimanche, nous
laissons notre voiture au **garage**.

garden n My friends have a beautiful **garden**.	**le jardin** [luh zhar•dehN] n Mes amis ont un beau **jardin**.
heating n The house had no **heating**.	**le chauffage** [luh shoh•fazh] n La maison n'avait pas de **chauffage**.
home n I have got a beautiful **home**.	**la maison; le foyer** [lah meh•zohN; luh fwah•yay] n J'ai une belle **maison**.
home adv I took the children **home** at 7:30 p.m.	**à la maison** [ah la meh•zohN] adv J'ai ramené les enfants **à la maison** à 19h30.
house n My **house** is on the other side of the hill.	**la maison** [lah meh•zohN] n Ma **maison** se trouve de l'autre côté de la colline.
key n Where is the **key**?	**la clé** [lah clay] n Où est **la clé?**
kitchen n She went into the **kitchen** to get something to drink.	**la cuisine** [lah kwee•zeen] n Elle est allée à **la cuisine** chercher quelque chose à boire.
lamp n She bought a new **lamp** for the living room.	**la lampe** [lah lawNp] n Elle a acheté une nouvelle **lampe** pour le salon.
lift n Brit. **elevator** n Am. You can use the **lift**.	**l'ascenseur** [lah•sawN•suhr] n Vous pouvez emprunter **l'ascenseur**.

light *n*
Please turn on the **light**.

la lumière [lah lew•mee•ehr] *n*
S'il te plaît, allume **la lumière**.

living room *n*
The children are in the
living room.

le salon [luh sah•lowN] *n*
Les enfants sont au **salon**.

to lock *v*

fermer à clé, verrouiller
[fehr•may ah clay, vay•roo•yay] *v*

Lock the door, please!
Ferme la porte **à clé**, s'il te plaît!

metal *n*
It's a **metal** door.

le métal [luh may•tahl] *n*
C'est une porte en **métal**.

to rent *v*
You can **rent** a car at the garage
at the top of the street.

louer [loo•ay] *v*
Vous pouvez **louer** une voiture au
garage au bout de la rue.

to repair *v*
Can you **repair** this for me,
please?

réparer [ray•pah•ray] *v*
Pouvez-vous me **réparer** ça,
s'il vous plaît?

room *n*

la pièce; la chambre
[lah pee•ess; lah shawN•bruh] *n*

Jack looked around the **room**.
Jack a parcouru **la pièce** du regard.

stairs *n pl*

les escaliers, l'escalier
[leh zes•kah•lee•yay,
lehs•kah•lee•yay] *n*

He went down the **stairs** to
open the door.
J'ai descendu **l'escalier** pour aller
ouvrir.

stuff *n*
They have old chairs and
that kind of **stuff**.

les trucs [leh trewk] *n*
Ils ont de vieilles chaises, et des
trucs du même genre.

table *n*	**la table** [lah ta·bluh] *n*
*Good evening, I've booked a **table** for four.*	*Bonsoir, j'ai réservé une **table** pour quatre.*
thing *n*	**la chose** [lah shoz] *n*
*He bought a lot of **things** we don't need.*	*Il a acheté plein de **choses** dont nous n'avons pas besoin.*
toilet *n Brit.*	**les toilettes, les WC** [leh twa·lett, leh vay·say] *n*
restroom *n Am.* *Where are the **toilets**?* *The **restroom** is downstairs.*	*Où sont les **toilettes**?* *Les **WC** sont en bas.*
washing machine *n*	**le lave-linge** [luh lahv·lehNzh] *n*
*This washing **machine** uses a lot of electricity.*	*Ce **lave-linge** consomme beaucoup d'énergie.*
window *n*	**la fenêtre** [lah fuh·neh·truh] *n*
*Please, close the **window**. It's getting cold in here.*	*S'il te plaît, ferme **la fenêtre**. Il commence à faire froid ici.*
wood *n*	**le bois** [luh bwah] *n*
*We have a **wooden** table in the kitchen.*	*Nous avons une table en **bois** dans la cuisine.*

Daily Routine

after *prep*
She always has a shower
***after** breakfast.*

après [ah•preh] *prep*
Elle prend toujours une douche
***après** le petit déjeuner.*

---

breakfast *n*

*Today we had **breakfast***
at 8:00 a.m.

le petit déjeuner
[luh puh•tee day•zhuh•nay] *n*
Aujourd'hui, nous avons pris
*notre **petit déjeuner** à huit heures.*

---

to close *v*
*Please, **close** the window!*

fermer [fayr•may] *v*
*Voulez-vous **fermer** la fenêtre,*
s'il vous plaît!

---

to cook *v*

*He was too ill **to cook** an*
evening meal.
*He can't **cook**.*

cuisiner, préparer, faire la
cuisine [kwee•zee•nay,
pray•pah•ray, fayr lah kwee•zeen] *v*
*Il était trop malade pour **préparer***
le dîner.
*Il ne sait pas **faire la cuisine**.*

---

dinner *n*
*We have **dinner** at six o'clock.*

le dîner [luh dee•nay] *n*
***Le dîner** est servi à dix-huit heures.*

---

to do *v*
*I've got nothing **to do** today.*

faire [fehr] *v*
*Je n'ai rien à **faire** aujourd'hui.*

---

early *adv*

*They came **early**.*
*They arrived **early**.*

tôt, en avance [toh, awN
nah•vawNs] *adv/loc*
*Ils sont arrivés **tôt**.*
*Ils sont arrivés **en avance**.*

---

first *adv*

d'abord, en premier
[dah•bor, awn pruh•mee•yay] *loc*

First I'll prepare dinner then I'll wash the dishes.	Je vais **d'abord** faire à manger, puis je laverai la vaisselle.
Which came **first**, the chicken or the egg?	Qu'est-ce qui est venu en **premier?** La poule ou l'œuf?
for *prep*	**depuis** [duh•pwee] *prep*
I've been living here **for** six years.	J'habite ici **depuis** six ans.
to get *v*	**prendre, aller chercher, acheter, recevoir** [prawN•druh, ah•lay shayr•shay, ash•tay, ruh•suh•vwar] *v*
Could you **get** me a Coke?	Pourrais-tu me **prendre** un Coca?
What did you **get** for Christmas?	Quels cadeaux as-tu **eus** à Noël?
to get dressed *loc*	**s'habiller** [sah•bee•yay] *v*
Get dressed! Breakfast is ready.	**Habille-toi!** Le petit déjeuner est servi.
to get up *v*	**se lever** [suh luh•vay] *v*
I **get up** at seven o'clock every day.	Je **me lève** à sept heures tous les jours.
to have *v*	**avoir** [ah•vwar] *v*
I don't **have** the time.	Je n'**ai** pas le temps.

Fact

You'll often hear the verb **avoir** used to form the past tense. For example: **J'ai mangé** – I have eaten.

to have a lie-in *loc*	**faire la grasse matinée** [fehr lah grahs mah•tee•nay] *loc*

On Saturdays I always have a **lie-in**.	Je fais toujours **la grasse matinée** les Samedis.
to have a shower *loc*	**prendre une douche** [prawN•druh ewn doosh] *loc*
I **have a shower** every night.	Je **prends une douche** tous les soirs.
to have to *v*	**devoir** [duh•vwar] *v*
I **have to** go home now.	Je **dois** rentrer chez moi.
housewife *n*	**la femme au foyer** [lah fahm oh fwa•yay] *n*
Why don't **housewives** get money for their work?	Pourquoi **les femmes au foyer** ne sont-elles pas payées pour leur travail?
to be hungry *loc*	**avoir faim** [ah•vwar fehN] *loc*
I'm getting **hungry** now.	Je commence à **avoir faim** maintenant.
late *adj*	**tard** [tahr] *adj*
It was very late **last** night when I came back.	Il était très **tard** la nuit dernière quand je suis rentré.
later *adv (comp. of late)*	**plus tard** [plew tahr] *loc*
See you **later**!	À **plus tard**!
to live *v*	**habiter** [ah•bee•tay] *v*
We **live** in a small flat on the fifth floor.	Nous **habitons** dans un petit appartement au cinquième étage.
lunch *n*	**le déjeuner** [luh day•zhuh•nay] *n*
What about a nice **lunch** in a pub?	Que dirais-tu de prendre un bon **déjeuner** au pub?

only adv

It's **only** eight o'clock.
Only you can do it.

seulement; seul
[suh•luh•mawN; suhl] adv

Il est **seulement** 8 (huit) heures.
Toi **seul** peux le faire.

to put away v
Please **put** your books away.

ranger [rawN•zhay] v
Range tes livres, s'il te plaît.

to put ... back v

She put the book **back**.
Did you remember to put the
clocks **back** last night?

**remettre en place, reposer;
retarder**
[ruh•may•truh awN plass,
ruh•poh•zay; ruh•tar•day] v

Elle a **remis** le livre en place.
As-tu pensé à **retarder** les horloges
hier soir?

shower n
Can I have a room with a
shower, please?

la douche [lah doosh] n
Pourrais-je avoir une chambre avec
douche, s'il vous plaît?

to sleep v
I couldn't **sleep** all night.

dormir [dor•meer] v
Je n'ai pas pu **dormir** de la nuit.

to stand v

She **stood** by the wall.
She **stood** in the garden and
listened to the birds.

**être debout, se tenir debout;
se tenir** [ay•truh duh•boo, suh
tuh•neer duh•boo; suh tuh•neer] v

Elle était **debout** près du mur.
Elle **se tenait** dans le jardin et
écoutait les oiseaux.

to stop v
He **stopped** the car.
He **stopped** smoking last year.

arrêter [ah•ray•tay] v
Il a **arrêté** la voiture.
Il a **arrêté** de fumer l'année dernière.

to take off *v*
Take off your shoes and then you can go into the house.

retirer [ruh·tee·ray] *v*
Retire tes chaussures et tu pourras entrer dans la maison.

---

to wait *v*
She stopped and **waited** for us.

attendre [ah·tawN·druh] *v*
Elle s'est arrêtée et nous a **attendus**.

---

to wake up *v*

Do the children sleep all night without **waking up**?
Why didn't you **wake** me up?

se réveiller; réveiller
[suh ray·vay·yay; ray·vay·yay] *v*
Les enfants dorment-ils toute la nuit sans **se réveiller**?
Pourquoi ne m'as-tu pas **réveillé**?

Clothes & Accessories

blouse *n*

That's a nice **blouse** you bought!

le chemisier
[luh shuh·mee·zee·yay] *n*
Il est joli **le chemisier** que tu as acheté!

---

to change *v*
I'm going out after work so I will have **to change**.

se changer [shawN·zhay] *v*
Je sors après le travail alors je vais devoir **me changer**.

---

clothes *n pl*
What kind of **clothes** do que you like best?

les vêtements [leh vett·mawN] *n*
Quel genre de **vêtements** est-ce tu préfères?

---

coat *n*
I want to buy a **coat**.

le manteau [luh mawN·toh] *n*
J'ai envie de m'acheter un **manteau**.

---

dress *n*
She chose a red **dress** for

la robe [lah rob] *n*
Elle a choisi une **robe** rouge pour

the party.	*aller à cette soirée.*
glasses *n pl*	**les lunettes** [leh lew•nett] *n*
*She's got nice **glasses**.*	*Elle a de jolies **lunettes**.*
it *pron neutre sg*	**il, elle; le, la l'; c'** [eel, ell; luh, lah l'; s'] *pron*
It's a lovely ring. It was my grand-mother's	*C'est une très jolie bague. **Elle** était à ma grand-mère.*
*Give **it** to me.*	*Donne-**le** moi. / Donne-**la** moi.*
*I don't like **it**.*	*Je ne **l**'aime pas.*
*He bought a coat and gave **it** to me.*	***Il** a acheté un manteau et me **l**'a donné.*
It is nice.	***C**'est beau.*
leather *n*	**le cuir** [luh kweer] *n*
*I saw a pair of nice **leather** shoes.*	*J'ai vu une belle paire de chaussures en **cuir**.*
pair *n*	**la paire** [lah pehr] *n*
*I need a new **pair** of black shoes.*	*J'ai besoin d'une nouvelle **paire** de chaussures noires.*
pullover *n*	**le pull** [luh pewl] *n*
*What a nice **pullover**!*	*Quel joli **pull**!*
purse *n Brit.*	**le porte-monnaie** [luh port•moh•neh] *n*
purse *n Am.*	**le sac à main** [le sac à main] *n*
*I put my tickets in my **purse**.*	*J'ai rangé mes tickets dans mon **porte-monnaie**.*
to put ... on *v*	**mettre** [may•truh] *v*
*That looks very nice, **put** it*	*C'est très joli, **mets**-le pour voir.*

58

on and let's have a look at you.

shirt n I need a clean **shirt**.	**la chemise** [lah shuh•meez] n Il me faut une **chemise** propre.
skirt n She gave all her **skirts** to her sister.	**la jupe** [lah zhewp] n Elle a donné toutes ses **jupes** à sa sœur.
shoe n I bought a new pair of **shoes** last week.	**la chaussure** [lah shoh•sewr] n J'ai acheté une nouvelle paire de **chaussures** la semaine dernière.
suit n That's a nice **suit** you bought yesterday.	**le costume** [luh koss•tewm] n Il est beau **le costume** que tu as acheté hier.
tights n pl Brit. **pantyhose** n Am. Where did you buy your new **tights**?	**le collant** [luh koh•lawN] n Où as-tu acheté ton nouveau **collant**?
trousers n pl Brit. **pants** n pl Am. I need a new pair of **trousers**.	**le pantalon** [luh pawN•tah•lohN] n J'ai besoin d'un nouveau **pantalon**.
to try on v Can I **try** this coat **on**?	**Essayer** [ay•say•yay] v Est-ce que je peux **essayer** ce manteau?
umbrella n Take an **umbrella** with you!	**le parapluie** [luh pah•rah•plwee] n Prends un **parapluie** en sortant!
wallet n	**le porte-feuille** [luh port•uh•fuh•yuh] n m

*Yesterday I bought a new **wallet**.* | *Hier, j'ai acheté un nouveau **porte-feuille**.*

---

wool *n*
*Is this pure **wool**?*

la laine [lah lenn] *n f*
*Est-ce que c'est de la pure **laine**?*

On the Move

about *adv*
*And then you walk for **about** two hundred metres.*

environ [awN·vee·rohN] *adv*
*Et ensuite vous marchez sur **environ** 200 mètres.*

---

airport *n*
*She lives very near the **airport**.*

l'aéroport [la·ay·roh·pohr] *n*
*Elle vit à proximité de l'**aéroport**.*

---

as *conj*
*I met Jane **as** I was getting off the bus.*

alors que [ah·lohr kuh] *loc*
*J'ai croisé Jane **alors que** je descendais de l'autobus.*

---

at *prep*
*Can we meet **at** the bus stop?*

à [ah] *prep*
*Pouvons-nous nous retrouver **à** l'arrêt d'autobus?*

---

bicycle *n*
*I bought a new **bicycle** yesterday.*

le vélo [luh vay·loh] *n m*
*J'ai acheté un nouveau **vélo** la semaine dernière.*

---

bus *n*

*We must park the car here and take the **bus**.*

le bus, l'autobus
[luh bews, loh·toh·bews] *n*
*Nous devons nous garer ici et prendre **le bus**.*

---

bus stop *n*

*I waited for him at the **bus stop**.*

l'arrêt d'autobus
[lah·reh doh·toh·bews] *n*
*Je l'ai attendu à l'**arrêt d'autobus**.*

class n A first-**class** ticket, please.	**la classe** [lah klass] n f Un billet de première **classe**, s'il vous plaît.
car n How did you get here? By **car**?	**la voiture, l'automobile** [lah vwa•tewr, loh•toh•moh• beel] n f Comment es-tu venu? En **voiture**?
car park n Brit. **parking lot** n Am. The new department store in the centre of town has a big **car park**.	**le parking** [luh par•king] n Le nouveau grand magasin en centre-ville a un immense **parking**.
departure n We met Jane a few hours after her brother's **departure** to Alaska.	**le départ** [luh day•pahr] n Nous avons rencontré Jane quelques heures après le **départ** de son frère en Alaska.
to drive v I'm learning to **drive**. Can we walk or do we have to **drive**?	**conduire; aller en voiture** [kohN•dweer; ah•lay awN vwa•tewr] v **J'apprends à conduire.** Est-ce qu'on peut y aller à pied ou bien faut-il y **aller en voiture**?
driving licence n Brit.	**le permis de conduire** [luh pair•mee duh kohN•dweer] n

driver's license n Am.
I need an international **driving licence**.

Il me faut un **permis de conduire** international.

ferry n
We took the **ferry** to France.

ferry [luh fay•ree] n
Nous avons pris le **ferry** pour aller en France.

flight n
Their **flight** arrives this evening.

le vol [luh vol] n
Leur **vol** arrive ce soir.

to fly v
A lot of birds **fly** south for the winter.

voler [voh•lay] v
Beaucoup d'oiseaux **volent** vers le sud en hiver.

garage n
Where can I find a **garage** near here?

le garage [luh gah•razh] n
Où pouvons-nous trouver un **garage** dans le coin?

to get v
How do I **get** to Kensington Road?

aller [ah•lay] v
Comment **va**-t-on à Kensington Road?

to get off v
Get off the bus at the station.

descendre [day•sawN•druh] v
Descends du bus à l'arrêt.

to get on v
We **got on** the train at Charing Cross.

monter [mohN•tay] v
Nous sommes **montés** dans le train à Charing Cross.

to go v
She **goes** to work by car.

aller [ah•lay] v`
Elle **va** au travail en voiture.

to land v
We **landed** at six o'clock.

atterrir [ah•tay•reer] v
Nous avons **atterri** à 6 (six) heures.

metre n Brit.
meter n Am.
The post office is about two
hundred **meters** from here.

le mètre [luh meh·truh] n

Le bureau de poste est à environ
deux cents **mètres** d'ici.

mile n

It's about half a **mile** down
the road on the left side.

le mile (équivalent à 1,609 km)
[luh mah·eel] n
C'est à environ un demi-**mile** d'ici,
sur la gauche.

noise n
I couldn't read because of the
noise of traffic.

le bruit [luh brwee] n
Je ne pouvais pas lire à cause du
bruit de la circulation.

oil n

Does your car use much **oil**?

l'huile (de vidange)
[lweel (duh vee·dawNzh)]
Est-ce que ta voiture consomme
beaucoup **d'huile**?

or conj
Did you walk **or** come by car?

ou [oo] conj
Es-tu venu à pied **ou** en voiture?

out adv
I want to go **out**.

dehors [duh·ohr] adv
Je veux aller **dehors**.

petrol n Brit.	**l'essence** [lay•sawNs] n
gas n Am.	
We don't have enough **petrol** to go to Brighton.	Nous n'avons pas assez d'**essence** pour aller jusqu'à Brighton.

plane n	**l'avion** [lah•vee•ohN] n
What time is your **plane** tomorrow?	À quelle heure est ton **avion** demain?

platform n Brit.	**la voie, le quai** [lah vwah, luh keh] n
track n Am.	
The train to Manchester arrives on **platform** five.	Le train pour Manchester entre en gare **voie** cinq.

private adj	**privé, e** [pree•vay, pree•vay] adj
You can't park here, it's a **private** parking space!	Vous ne pouvez pas vous garer ici, c'est un parking **privé**!

railroad n Am.	**Le chemin de fer** [luh shuh•mehN duh fehr] n
The road runs parallel to the **railway**.	La route longe la voie de **chemin de fer**.

Fact

You use **la rue** to refer to a street such as in a town or city, while route is a major road between towns such as a highway.
See p. 65.

road n
*Is this the **road** to Bath?*

la route [lah root] n
*Est-ce que je suis bien sur **la route** de Bath?*

round prep
*You go **round** the corner and follow the signs for Dover.*

tourner [toor•nay] v
***Tournez** au coin de la rue et suivez les panneaux indiquant Douvres.*

sign n
*Didn't she see the stop **sign**?*

le panneau [luh pah•noh] n
*Elle n'a pas vu **le panneau** de stop?*

street n
*They crossed the **street** at a pedestrian crossing.*

la rue [lah rew] n
*Ils ont traversé **la rue** au passage piéton.*

taxi n
*We had to take a **taxi**. There was no bus to our hotel.*

le taxi [luh tak•see] n
*Nous avons dû prendre un **taxi**. Aucun autobus ne desservait notre hôtel.*

there adv
*How can we get **there**?*

là, là-bas [lah, lah bah] adv
*Comment pouvons-nous nous rendre **là-bas**?*

to prep
*Which road do I take **to** Bath?*

à [ah] prep
*Quelle route dois-je prendre pour aller **à** Bath?*

station n
*How far is it to the **station**?*

la gare [lah gahr] n
*Est-ce que **la gare** est loin?*

ticket n
*Two **tickets**, please.*

le billet [luh bee•yeh] n
*Deux **billets**, s'il vous plaît.*

timetable n Brit. **schedule** n Am. Have you got the **timetable**?	**l'horaire** [loh•rehr] n Avez-vous un **horaire** à me donner?
traffic lights n Why didn't you stop at the **traffic lights**?	**les feux de signalisation, le feu (rouge)** [lay fuh duh see•nee•ah•lee •zah•syohN, luh fuh (roozh)] n Pourquoi ne t'es-tu pas arrêté au **feu** rouge?
train n What time does the **train** go?	**le train** [luh trehN] n À quelle heure part **le train**?
tram n How did you get here? By **tram**?	**le tramway** [luh tramm•way] n Comment es-tu venu? Par le **tramway**?
tyre n Brit. **tire** n Am. I have to buy some new **tyres** for my car.	**le pneu** [luh pnuh] n J'ai besoin de nouveaux **pneus** pour ma voiture.
to walk v Let's **walk** a little faster!	**marcher** [mar•shay] v **Marchons** un peu plus vite!
way n Could you tell us the **way** to the station, please?	**le chemin** [luh shuh•mehN] n Pouvez-vous nous indiquer **le chemin** jusqu'à la gare?
yard n And then you walk for about two hundred **yards**.	**le yard** [luh yard] n Ensuite, vous marchez sur environ 200 **yards**.

Asking for Directions

above *prep*

Our flat is **above** a pub.

au-dessus de
[oh duh•sew duh] *loc*
Notre appartement se trouve
au-dessus d'un pub.

---

at the back *loc*

There's a car park **at the back**
of the cinema.

à l'arrière de, derrière
[ah lah•ree•ehr duh, deh•ree•ehr] *loc*
Il y a un parking **derrière** la salle
de cinéma.

---

at the bottom *loc*
Look **at the bottom** of
page thirty.

en bas [awN bah] *loc*
Regarde **en bas** de la page trente.

---

at the front *loc*

We are sitting **at the front**.

à l'avant, devant
[ah lah•vawN, duh•vawN] *loc*
Nous sommes assis **devant**.

---

back *adj*

The **back** door is closed.

de derrière, arrière
[duh deh•ree•ehr, ah•ree•ehr] *loc*
La porte **de derrière** est fermée.

---

behind *prep*
There was a bus **behind** my car.

derrière [deh•ree•ehr] *prep*
Il y avait un bus **derrière** ma
voiture.

---

between *prep*
The hotel was **between** the
station and the centre of town.

entre [awN•truh] *prep*
Notre hôtel se trouvait **entre** la
gare et le centre-ville.

---

can *v*
Can you tell me how to get
to this place?

pouvoir [poo•vwar] *v*
Pouvez-vous me dire comment aller
à cet endroit?

Do ...? *v*
Do you know the way to the
station?

Savez-vous comment aller
à la gare?

---

down *adv*
Go **down** the road for about
half a mile.

descendre [day•sawN•druh] *v*
Descendez la route sur environ un
demi-mile.

---

downstairs *adv*
The bedroom is **downstairs**.

en bas [awN bah] *loc*
La chambre est **en bas**.

---

east *n*
Which way is **east**?

l'est [lest] *n*
De quel côté se trouve **l'est?**

---

east *adv*
Is that **east** of here?

à l'est (de) [ah lest (duh)] *loc*
Est-ce que c'est **à l'est** d'ici?

Fact

The four cardinal points **nord**, **sud**, **est** and **ouest** can also be
written with an initial capital letter.

---

far *adj*
Is it **far** from here?

loin [loo•ehN] *adj*
Est-ce que c'est **loin** d'ici?

---

front *adj*

devant, à l'avant de
[duh•vawN, ah lah•vawN duh] *loc*

I went to the **front** of
the building.

Je suis allé **à l'avant** du bâtiment.

---

here *adv*
There are no children **here**.

ici [ee•see] *adv*
Il n'y a pas d'enfants **ici**.

into prep
Please go **into** the office and wait there.

dans [dawN] prep
Veuillez entrer **dans** le bureau et patienter.

---

kilometre n Brit.

kilometer n Am.
We live in a small town about a hundred **kilometers** west of London.

le kilomètre [luh kee•loh•meh•truh] n

Nous habitons dans une petite ville à environ cent **kilomètres** de Londres.

---

left n
The bank's to the **left** of the post office.

gauche [gohsh] n
La banque se trouve à **gauche** du bureau de poste.

---

metre n Brit.
meter n Am.
The post office is about two hundred **meters** from here.

le mètre [luh meh•truh] n

Le bureau de poste est à environ deux cents **mètres** d'ici.

---

middle n
Don't drive in the **middle** of the road!

le milieu [luh mee•lee•uh] n
Ne roule pas au **milieu** de la route!

---

near prep
Joan's flat is **near** the station.

près [preh] prep
L'appartement de Joan se trouve **près** de la gare.

---

north n
How far **north** can I go?

le nord [luh nor] n
Jusqu'où puis-je aller en direction du **nord?**

---

north adv
Philadelphia is **north**

au nord (de) [oh nor (duh)] loc
Philadelphie est **au nord de**

of Baltimore. | Baltimore.

nowhere *adv*
Where did you go last night?
– **Nowhere.** We stayed at home.

nulle part [newl par] *loc*
Où êtes-vous allés hier soir?
– **Nulle part.** Nous sommes restés
à la maison.

on *prep*
Put the potatoes **on** the table.

sur [sewr] *prep*
Mets les pommes de terre **sur**
la table.

out *prep*
She walked **out** of the room.

sortir [sohr•teer] *v*
Elle est **sortie** de la pièce.

outside *adv*
It was almost dark **outside**.

dehors [duh•ohr] *adv*
Il faisait presque nuit **dehors**.

over *prep*
There's a bridge **over** the river.

au-dessus de [oh duh•sew duh] *loc*
Un pont passe **au-dessus de** la
rivière.

right *adj*
Do you write with your **right**
or your left hand?

droit, e [drwa, drwat] *adj*
Est-ce que tu écris de la main **droite**
ou de la main gauche?

side *n*
The post office is on the
right **side**.

côté [koh•tay] *n*
Le bureau de poste est du **côté** droit
de la rue.

south *n*
We live in the **south** of the city.

le sud [luh sewd] *n*
Nous vivons dans **le sud** de la ville.

south *adv*
Our village is **south** of
Nottingham.

au sud (de) [oh sewd (duh)] *loc*
Notre village est **au sud de**
Nottingham.

through *prep*
I went **through** the door into the garden.

franchir [frawN•sheer] *v*
J'ai **franchi** la porte pour aller dans le jardin.

top *n*

We couldn't see the mountain **top**.
She waited for me at the **top** of the stairs.

le haut; en haut de
[luh oh; awN oh duh] *n*
On ne voyait pas **le haut** de la montagne.
Elle m'a attendu **en haut des** escaliers.

under *prep*
The dog is **under** the table.

sous [soo] *prep*
Le chien est **sous** la table.

up *prep*
We walked **up** the street.
His new house is up in the mountains.

remonter [ruh•mohN•tay] *v*
Nous avons **remonté** la rue.
Sa nouvelle maison est perchée dans la montagne.

upstairs *adv*
The toilet's **upstairs**.

en haut [awN oh] *loc*
Les toilettes sont **en haut**.

west *n*
The wind is blowing from the **west**.

l'ouest [lwest] *n*
Le vent vient de **l'ouest**.

west *adv*
Bath is **west** of London.

à l'ouest (de) [ah lwest (duh)] *loc*
Bath se situe **à l'ouest** de Londres.

wide *adj*
The road was not **wide** enough for the bus.
I want to see the big **wide** world.

large; vaste [larzh; vast] *adj*
La route n'était pas assez **large** pour le bus.
Je veux découvrir le **vaste** monde.

wrong *adj*	**mauvais, e**
	[moh•veh, moh•vehz] *adj*
Excuse me. You're going the	*Pardon, mais vous allez dans la*
***wrong** way.*	***mauvaise** direction.*

School & Study

at first *loc*	**au début** [oh day•bew] *loc*
At first, I didn't like my	*Au début, je n'aimais pas ma*
new school.	*nouvelle école.*
class *n*	**la classe** [lah klass] *n*
*The **class** has twenty pupils.*	*Il y a vingt élèves dans **la classe**.*
could not, couldn't *v*	**ne pas pouvoir**
	[nuh pah poo•vwar] *v*
*I **couldn't** do the maths exercise.*	*Je **n'ai pas** pu faire l'exercice de maths.*

Fact

Before a vowel (a,e,i,o,u) or a silent h the short form **n'** is used instead of **ne**. In spoken French it is often even omitted entirely: **Je sais pas** – I don't know.

course *n*	**le cours** [luh koor] *n*
*I am enrolled in a French **course**.*	*Je suis inscrit dans un **cours** de français.*
to explain *v*	**expliquer** [ex•plee•kay] *v*
*Can you **explain** it to me?*	*Pourriez-vous m'**expliquer** ça?*

to forget *v*
I've **forgotten** everything I learned at school.

oublier [oo·blee·yay] *v*
J'ai **oublié** tout ce que j'ai appris a l'école.

---

to hope *v*
I **hope** I pass my exams!

espérer [es·pay·ray] *v*
J'**espère** que je réussis mes examens!

---

to know *v*

Do you **know** your poem by heart?
Did you **know** that?

connaître; savoir
[kon·nay·truh; sah·vwar] *v*
Est-ce que tu **connais** ton poème par cœur?
Tu **savais** ça?

---

to learn *v*
How many languages did you **learn** at school?

apprendre [ah·prawN·druh] *v*
Combien de langues as-tu **apprises** à l'école?

---

mistake *n*
I still make a lot of **mistakes**.

la faute [lah foht] *n*
Je fais encore beaucoup de **fautes**.

---

must *v*
You **must** do your homework tonight after dinner.

devoir [duh·vwar] *v*
Tu dois faire tes **devoirs** ce soir après le dîner.

---

pen *n*
Can you lend me your **pen**?

le stylo [luh stee·loh] *n*
Peux-tu me prêter ton **stylo**?

---

pencil *n*
Do you want a pen or a **pencil**?

le crayon [luh kreh·yohN] *n*
Préfères-tu un stylo ou un **crayon**?

---

to promise *v*
I **promise** to do my homework after dinner.

promettre [pro·may·truh] *v*
Je **promets** de faire mes devoirs après le dîner.

school n
I go to **school** every morning
at eight.

l'école [lay·kohl] n
Je vais à **l'école** tous les matins à
8 (huit) heures.

since prep
I've been **studying** English
since January.

depuis [duh·pwee] prep
J'étudie l'anglais **depuis** Janvier.

start n
That's a good **start**.

début [day·bew] n
C'est un bon **début**!

student n

How many **students** were there
on the course?

l'étudiant, e
[lay·tew·dee·awN,
lay·tew·dee·awNt] n
Combien y avait-il **d'étudiants**
dans ta classe?

to take v
Which course are you **taking**
next year?

prendre [prawN·druh] v
Quelle option **prends-tu** l'année
prochaine?

teacher n

What do you think of our
new **teacher**?

le professeur
[luh proh·fay·suhr] n
Que penses-tu de notre nouveau
professeur?

test n The **test** was not very difficult.	**le contrôle** [luh kohN•trohl] n *Le contrôle n'était pas très difficile.*
timetable n Brit.	**l'emploi du temps** [lawN•plwa dew tawN] n
schedule n Am. Is this your **timetable**?	*Est-ce que c'est ton **emploi du temps**?*
university n She wants to go to **university** next year.	**l'université** [lew•nee•vehr•see•tay] n *Elle veut aller à **l'université** l'année prochaine.*
to use v Can I **use** your dictionary?	**utiliser** [ew•tee•lee•zay] v *Est-ce que je peux **utiliser** votre dictionnaire?*

Official Business

bank n Where can I find a **bank** near here?	**la banque** [lah bawNk] n *Où puis-je trouver une **banque** dans le coin?*
boss n What's your new **boss** like?	**le/la chef** [luh /lah shehf] n *Comment est ta nouvelle **chef**?*

to bring back *v*
***Bring** back your documents next week.*

Rapporter [rah•por•tay] *v*
***Rapportez** vos documents la semaine prochaine.*

busy *adj*

occupé, e
[oh•kew•pay, oh•kew•pay] *adj*

*I'm very **busy** at the moment.*

*Je suis très **occupé** en ce moment.*

computer *n*
*Can you work with a **computer**?*

l'ordinateur [lohr•dee•nah•tuhr] *n*
*Sais-tu te servir d'un **ordinateur**?*

to earn *v*
*How much do you **earn** a month?*

gagner [gah•nyay] *v*
*Combien **gagnes**-tu par mois?*

embassy *n*
*We're looking for the **embassy**.*

l'embassade [lawn•bahs•ahd] *n*
*On cherche l'**embassade** de France.*

employee *n*
I met the new employee today.

l'employé [lawn•plwah•yay] *m n*
*J'ai rencontré le nouvel **employé**.*

to fill in *v Brit.*

remplir, compléter
[rawN•pleer, kohN•pleh•tay] *v*

to fill out *v Am.*
*Could you help me (to) **fill in** this form?*

*Pouvez-vous m'aider à **remplir** ce formulaire?*

firm *n*

la société, l'entreprise
[lah soh•see•ay•tay, lawN•truh•preez] *n*

*I work for a small **firm**.*

*Je travaille pour une petite **entreprise**.*

form *n*	**le formulaire** [luh for•mew•lehr] *n*
*Please fill in this **form**.*	*Veuillez remplir ce **formulaire**.*
to go to work *loc*	**aller travailler** [ah•lay trah•vah•yay] *loc*
*What time do you go to **work** in the morning?*	*A quelle heure vas-tu **travailler** le matin?*
insurance *n* *How much is your car **insurance**?*	**l'assurance** [lah•sew•rawNs] *f n* *Combien coûte **l'assurance** de ta voiture?*
job *n*	**le travail, l'emploi** [luh trah•vahy, lawN•plwah] *n*
*I think he has found the right **job**.* *I have a new **job**.*	*Je crois qu'il a trouvé **le travail** qu'il lui fallait.* *J'ai un nouvel **emploi**.*
lawyer *n*	**l'avocat, e** [lah•voh•kah, lah•voh•katt] *n*
*We know a good **lawyer**.*	*Nous connaissons un bon **avocat**.*
library *n*	**la bibliothèque** [lah bee•blee•yoh•tehk] *n*
*I'm sure you can find that book in the **library**.*	*J'en suis sûre que vous trouverez ce livre dans **la bibliothèque**.*
manager *n*	**le/la responsable** [luh/ lah ress•pohN•sah•bluh] *n*
*She's the **manager** of a small firm.*	*Elle est **responsable** d'une petite entreprise.*
moment *n*	**en ce moment** [awN suh moh•mawN] *loc*

I don't have any time at the **moment**.	Je n'ai pas le temps **en ce moment**.
office n	**le bureau** [luh bew•roh] n
I'm not at the **office** at the moment. Please call later.	Je ne suis pas dans mon **bureau** actuellement. Veuillez rappeler plus tard.
Our **office** will be closed. next Friday	Nos **bureaux** seront fermés vendredi prochain.
post n Brit. **mail** n Am.	**le courrier** [luh koo•ree•ay] n
I received a lot of **post** this morning.	J'avais beaucoup de **courrier** ce matin.
post office n	**le bureau de poste** [luh bew•roh duh post] n
Is there a **post office** around here?	Est-ce qu'il y a un **bureau de poste** dans le coin?
to send v	**envoyer, poster** [awN•vwa•yay, pos•tay] v
Did you **send** that postcard?	As-tu **envoyé** cette carte postale?
to sign v	**signer** [see•nee•yay] v
Would you please **sign** here?	Voulez-vous bien **signer** ici?
signature n	**la signature** [lah see•nyah•tewr] n
We need a **signature** here.	On a besoin d'une **signature** ici.
stamp n	**le timbre** [luh tehN•bruh] n
Can I have a **stamp** for this letter to Australia, please?	Je voudrais un **timbre** pour envoyer cette lettre en Australie, s'il vous plaît?

Fact

If you want to buy stamps while you are in France, you would find these in a **Tabac store**. This is also where you would go to buy cigarettes and tobacco.

---

to start *v*
What time do you **start** work in the morning?

commencer [koh·mawN·say] *v*
A quelle heure **commences-tu** ton travail le matin?

---

urgent *adj*

There's an **urgent** call for Mr Thomas.

urgent, e
[ewr·zhawN, ewr·zhawNt] *adj*
Il y a un appel **urgent** pour M. Thomas.

---

will *v*
He **will** be in a meeting tomorrow. Il **sera** en réunion demain.

---

work *n*
Do you like this kind of **work**?

le travail [luh trah·vahy] *n*
Est-ce que tu aimes ce gènre de **travail?**

---

to work *v*
She **works** as a teacher.

travailler [trah·va·yay] *v*
Elle **travaille** comme enseignante.

Communicating

about *prep*
The women argued **about** money.

à propos [ah proh·poh] *loc*
Les femmes se disputaient **à propos** d'argent.

---

all right *loc*
It's **all right**.

d'accord [dah·kohr] *loc*
C'est **d'accord**.

answerphone n Brit.

le répondeur (téléphonique)
[luh ray·pohN·duhr
(tay·lay·foh·neek)] n

answering machine n Am.
I've left a message on your **answerphone.**

Je t'ai laissé un message sur ton **répondeur**.

by prep
Why don't you send it **by** email?

par [pahr] prep
Pourquoi ne pas le lui envoyer **par** e-mail?

Bye! interj

Au revoir! Salut!
[oh ruh·vwar sah·lew] interj

Bye, see you later.

Au revoir, à tout à l'heure!

to call v
And then we went outside and **called** the police.

appeler [ah·puh·lay] v
Alors nous sommes sortis et avons **appelé** la police.

card n

la carte de vœux
[lah kahrt duh vuh] n

We always get a lot of **cards** at Christmas.

Nous recevons toujours beaucoup de **cartes de vœux** à Noël.

to communicate v

correspondre
[koh·ress·pohN·druh] v

When I'm on holiday we must **communicate** by email.

Quand je serai en vacances, nous devrons **correspondre** par e-mail.

dear adj
Dear Mary, . . .

cher, chère [shehr, shehr] adj
Chère Mary, . . .

to email v

envoyer un e-mail
[awN·vwa·yay uhN ee·mail] v

*Please call, write or **email** me soon.*

*S'il te plaît, appelle, écris ou **envoie-moi vite un e-mail**.*

Excuse me *interj*
***Excuse me**, please, but this is my plate.*

Pardon [pahr·dohN] *interj*
***Pardon**, mais c'est mon assiette.*

for *prep*
*I've got a letter **for** you.*

pour [poor] *prep*
*J'ai une lettre **pour** toi.*

from *prep*
*Yesterday I got an email **from** my father.*

de [duh] *prep*
*Hier, j'ai reçu un e-mail **de** mon père.*

to get *v*
*I **got** twenty emails last weekend.*

recevoir [ruh·suh·vwar] *v*
*J'ai **reçu** vingt e-mails le week-end dernier.*

to be going to *loc*
*I'm **going to** write that email tomorrow.*

aller [a·lay] *v*
*Je **vais** écrire cet e-mail demain.*

Goodbye *loc*
***Goodbye**, Anne, see you next week.*

Au revoir [oh ruh·vwar] *loc*
***Au revoir**, Anne, à la semaine prochaine.*

Good afternoon *loc*
***Good afternoon**. Can I help you?*

Bonjour [bohN·zhoor] *interj*
***Bonjour**, en quoi puis-je vous aider?*

Good evening *loc*
***Good evening**. Welcome to our party.*

Bonsoir [bohN·swahr] *interj*
***Bonsoir**. Bienvenue à notre fête.*

Good morning *loc*
***Good morning**. Nice to see you!*

Bonjour [bohN·zhoor] *interj*
***Bonjour**. Content de te voir!*

Hello *interj*
Hello Chris. How are things?

Salut [sah·lew] *interj*
Salut, Chris. Comment ça va?

Hi *interj fam*
Hi! How are you?

Salut [sah·lew] *interj*
Salut, ça va?

I'm afraid... *loc*

Je crains..., Je regrette...
[zhuh krehN...,
zhuh ruh·grett...] *loc*

I'm afraid I can't help you.

Je crains de ne pas pouvoir vous
aider.

Internet *n*
I found my last job on
the **Internet**.

Internet [ehN·tayr·nett] *n*
J'ai trouvé mon dernier emploi sur
Internet.

It doesn't matter. *loc*

Ça ne fait rien.
[sah nuh fay ree·yehN.] *loc*

We're all having the same thing,
so **it doesn't matter**.

Ça ne fait rien, puisque nous
prenons tous la même chose.

letter *n*
He wrote a **letter** and explained
everything.

la lettre [lah leh·truh] *n*
Il a écrit une **lettre** dans laquelle il
expliquait tout.

Look out! *Interj*

Attention
[ah·tawN·see·yohN] *interj*

Look out! There's a car coming.

Attention! Une voiture arrive.

magazine *n*
Is this a women's **magazine**?

le magazine [luh mah·gah·zeen] *n*
Est-ce que c'est un **magazine**
féminin?

mobile phone *n*	**le (téléphone) portable** [luh (tay·lay·fonn) por·tah·bluh] *n*
cellphone *n Am.*	
Why didn't you call me on my **mobile phone**?	Pourquoi ne m'as-tu pas appelé sur mon **portable**?

news *n sg*	**les nouvelles; les informations** [leh noo·vell; leh zehN·for·mah·see·ohN] *n*
I've got some important **news** for you.	J'ai de grandes **nouvelles** pour toi.
Have you heard the **news** today?	As-tu écouté **les informations** aujourd'hui?
newspaper, paper *n*	**le journal** [luh zhoor·nahl] *n*
Can I have a look at your **newspaper**?	Je peux lire ton **journal?**
Nice to meet you. *Loc*	**Enchanté, e.** [awN·shawN·tay, awN·shawN·tay] *(de vous rencontrer) adj*
Hello, I'm Alina Jones. **Nice to meet you**.	Bonjour, je m'appelle Alina Jones. **Enchantée**.
no *adv*	**non** [nohN] *adv*
The answer is **no**.	La réponse est **non**.
not *adv*	**ne...pas** [nuh...pah] *adv*
Holland is small, it's **not** a big country.	Les Pays-Bas **ne sont pas** un grand pays.
You're **not** old enough to drive a car.	Tu **n'as pas** l'âge de conduire une voiture.

okay *adj abbr* OK
Do you need help?
*— No, thanks, I'm **okay**.*

ça va [sah vah] *loc*
Vous avez besoin d'aide?
*— Non, **ça va**, merci.*

---

page *n*
*The book has three hundred and sixty-four **pages**.*

la page [lah pazh] *n*
*Le livre a trois cent soixante-quatre **pages**.*

---

paper *n*

le papier; le journal
[luh pah•pee•yay;
luh zhoor•nahl] *n*

*She writes her letters on yellow **paper**.*
*Is there anything interesting in today's **paper**?*

*Elle écrit son courrier sur du **papier** jaune.*
*Est-ce qu'il y a des nouvelles intéressantes dans **le journal** aujourd'hui?*

Pardon? *interj*

Pardon? I didn't understand that.

Pardon? / Comment?
[pahr•dohN?, koh•mawN?] *interj*
***Comment?** Je n'ai pas compris.*

---

to phone *v*
*Why don't you **phone** your brother?*

téléphoner [tay•lay•foh•nay] *v*
*Pourquoi ne **téléphones-tu** pas à ton frère?*

---

to phone back *v*
*Thank you for **phoning back**.*

rappeler [rah•puh•lay] *v*
*Merci de me **rappeler**.*

---

please *interj*
*Can I have some tea, **please**?*

s'il vous plaît [seel•voo•play] *loc*
*Pourrais-je avoir du thé, **s'il vous plaît**?*

You say **s'il vous plaît** to be polite in a formal setting or when you are talking to someone older or that you do not know. To be less formal, you can say **s'il te plaît**. This applies if you are talking to friends, someone your own age or a person that you know well.

postcard *n*

la carte postale
[lah kahrt poh•stahl] *n*

*I'm going to send this **postcard** to her mother.*

*Je vais envoyer cette **carte postale** à sa mère.*

private *adj*

confidentiel, elle
[kohN•fee•dawN•see•ell] *adj*

*This is a **private** letter.*

*Cette lettre est **confidentielle**.*

programme *n Brit.*
program *n Am.*

l'émission [lay•mee•see•yohN] *n*

*There's a good **program** on TV tonight.*

*Il y a une bonne **émission** à la télévision ce soir.*

radio *n*

la radio [lah ra•dee•oh] *n*

*Did you hear the news on the **radio**?*

*As-tu entendu les nouvelles à **la radio**?*

to repeat *v*

répéter [ray•pay•tay] *v*

*Could you **repeat** that, please?*

*Pouvez-vous **répéter**, s'il vous plaît?*

to say goodbye *loc*

dire au revoir
[deer oh ruh•vwar] *loc*

*Mike, **say goodbye** to Lisa, we're going home now.*

*Mike, dis **au revoir** à Lisa, nous rentrons chez nous maintenant.*

See you soon! *loc*	**A bientôt!; A tout à l'heure!** [ah bee•ehN•toh; Ah too•tah•luhr] *loc*
so *adv* I hope **so**, but I don't think **so**.	Je l'espère, mais je n'y crois pas.
Sorry! *interj* Oh, have I taken your pen? **Sorry!**	**Désolé!** [day•zoh•lay] *interj* Oh, je vous ai pris votre stylo? **Désolé!**
Sorry? *interj* **Sorry?** – Oh, it was nothing important.	**Pardon?** [pahr•dohN] *interj* **Pardon?** – Oh, ce n'était rien d'important.
to speak *v* How many languages do you **speak**?	**parler** [pahr•lay] *v* Combien de langues **parlez-vous**?
to spell *v* How do you **spell** this name?	**épeler** [ay•puh•lay] *v* Comment **épelles-tu** ce nom?
sure *adj* I don't know, I'm not **sure**.	**sûr, e** [sewr, sewr] *adj* Je ne sais pas, je ne suis pas **sûr**.
Sure! *interj* Yes, **sure!** Let's go!	**bien sûr, d'accord** [bee•ehN sewr, dah•kohr] *interj* Oui, **bien sûr!** Allons-y!
talk *n* We had a **talk** about money.	**la discussion** [lah dees•kew•see•yohN] *n* Nous avons eu une **discussion** à propos d'argent.

to talk v	**parler, discuter** [pahr·lay, dees·kew·tay] v
We are **talking** about the news.	Nous **parlons** de questions d'actualité.

telephone n	**le téléphone** [luh tay·lay·fonn] n
She's always on the **telephone**.	Elle est toujours pendue au **téléphone**.

text message n	**le SMS, le texto** [luh ess·emm·ess, luh tex·toh] n
Why don't you send her a **text message**?	Pourquoi ne lui envoies-tu pas un **SMS?**

Thank you! loc	**Merci!** [mehr·see] interj
Thank you very much. That was very kind of you.	**Merci** infiniment. C'était très aimable à vous.

to translate v	**traduire** [trah·dweer] v
Could you **translate** this letter for me, please?	Pourrais-tu me **traduire** cette lettre, s'il te plaît?

to understand v	**comprendre** [kohN·prawN·druh] v
Sorry, I don't **understand**.	Pardon, mais je ne **comprends** pas.

Welcome! Interj	**Bienvenue!** [bee·ehN·vuh·new] interj
Welcome to Wales! **Welcome** home!	**Bienvenue** au pays de Galles! **Bienvenue** au pays!

You're welcome! loc	**De rien!; Je vous en prie!** [duh ree·yehN; zhuh voo zawN pree] loc

Thank you very much.
— **You're welcome**.

Merci beaucoup. — *Je vous en prie*.

---

to be welcome *loc*

**être le bienvenu, être
la bienvenue**
[ay•truh luh bee•ehN•vuh•new,
ay•truh lah bee•ehN•vuh•new] *loc*

You're always **welcome**.

*Vous êtes toujours **le bienvenu**.*

---

well *interj*
Well, do you want to have
the red dress or not?

eh bien [ay bee•yehN] *interj*
*Eh bien, tu la veux cette robe rouge,
oui ou non?*

What …! *interj*

Quel…!, Quelle…!
[kayl, kayl] *interj*

What a beautiful night!

Quelle belle nuit!

---

to write *v*
Can your son **write**?

Ecrire [ay•creer] *v*
*Votre fils sait-il **écrire**?*

---

to write down *v*
Can you **write** the address down
for me, please?

Noter [noh•tay] *S*
*Peux-tu **noter** cette adresse pour
moi, s'il te plaît?*

---

yes *adv*
Yes, certainly.

oui [wee] *adv*
Oui, bien sûr.

Leisure

Food

apple *n*
She bought a pound of **apples.**

la pomme [lah pohm] *n*
Elle a acheté une livre de **pommes**.

beef *n*
Would you like **beef** or pork?

le bœuf [luh buhf] *n*
Que préfères-tu? Du **bœuf** ou du porc?

biscuit *n Brit.*
cookie *n Am.*
I like chocolate **cookies** best.

le biscuit [luh bis•kwee] *n*

Mes préférés, ce sont les **biscuits** au chocolat.

bread *n*
I like **bread** with butter and cheese.

le pain [luh pehN] *n*
J'aime **le pain** avec du beurre et du fromage.

croissant *n*
*I usually have a **croissant**
for breakfast.*

le croissant [luh krwah•sawN] *n*
*Je mange d'habitude un **croissant**
au petit déjeuner.*

cake *n*
*Did you buy that **cake** or
did your brother buy it?*

le gâteau [luh gah•toh] *n*
*C'est toi ou ton frère qui a acheté ce
gâteau?*

Fact

In **la boulangerie** you can buy mainly bread, while in **la pâtisserie**
you'll find cakes and pastries.

---

cheese *n*
*Monterey Jack is an American
cheese.*

le fromage [luh froh•mazh] *n*
*Le Monterey Jack est un **fromage**
américain.*

chicken *n*
***Chicken** and chips, please.*

le poulet [luh poo•leh] *n*
*Un **poulet** avec des frites,
s'il vous plaît.*

chocolate *n*
*I like **chocolate**.*

le chocolat [luh sho•koh•lah] *n*
*J'aime **le chocolat**.*

dessert *n*
*What **dessert** will you have?*

dessert [luh deh•sehr] *n*
*Quel **dessert** prendrez-vous?*

to eat *v*
*She's **eating** an apple.*

manger [mawN•zhay] *v*
*Elle **mange** une pomme.*

egg *n*
*I always have an **egg** for
breakfast at the weekend.*

l'œuf [luhf] *n*
*Je prends toujours un **œuf** au petit
déjeuner le week-end.*

fish n We had **fish** for lunch.	**le poisson** [luh pwa•sohN] n Nous avons mangé du **poisson** au déjeuner.
food n He only eats organic **food**.	**la nourriture** [lah noo•ree•tewr] n Il ne mange que de la **nourriture** bio.
fruit n You must eat lots of **fruit** and vegetables.	**le fruit** [luh frwee] n Il faut manger beaucoup de **fruits** et de légumes.
ham n She made a **ham** and cheese salad.	**le jambon** [luh zhawN•bohN] n Elle a préparé une salade au **jambon** et au fromage.
hamburger n I don't like **hamburgers**.	**le hamburger** [luh hawN•buhr•guhr] n Je n'aime pas les **hamburgers**.
lamb n There's beef, pork or **lamb** for lunch.	**l'agneau** [lah•nee•oh] n Il y a du bœuf, du porc ou de **l'agneau** au déjeuner.
meat n I don't eat **meat**. I don't like it.	**la viande** [lah vi•awNd] n Je ne mange pas de **viande**. Je n'aime pas ça.
piece n I'd like a **piece** of that cake, please.	**le morceau** [luh mohr•soh] n Je prendrai un **morceau** de ce gâteau, s'il vous plaît.
pork n In many countries people don't eat **pork**.	**le porc** [luh pohr] n Dans beaucoup de pays, les gens ne mangent pas de **porc**.

Fact

In **la boucherie** you can buy mainly beef, while in **la charcuterie** you'll find pork and various types of sausage.

potato *n*	**la pomme de terre** [lah pohm duh tehr] *n*
*How many **potatoes** do you need?*	*Combien de **pommes de terre** voulez-vous?*
salad *n*	**la salade** [lah sah•lad] *n*
*How about a potato **salad**?*	*Que dirais-tu d'une **salade** de pommes de terre?*
sandwich *n*	**le sandwich** [luh sawNd•weetsh] *n*
*I wasn't very hungry, so I had a **sandwich** at lunchtime.*	*Je n'avais pas très faim, alors j'ai mangé un **sandwich** au déjeuner.*
snack *n*	**l'encas** [lawN•kah] *m n*
*I only have a **snack** for lunch.*	*Je ne prends qu'un **encas** au déjeuner.*
soup *n*	**la soupe** [lah soop] *n*
*We started the meal with chicken **soup**.*	*Nos avons mangé une **soupe** de poulet en entrée.*
steak *n*	**le steak, le bifteck** [luh stehk, luh beef•tehk] *n*
*How do you eat your **steak**?*	*Quelle cuisson pour ton **steak**?*
toast *n*	**le pain grillé** [luh pehN gree•yay] *n*
*One piece of **toast** or two?*	*Veux-tu une ou deux tartines de **pain grillé**?*

vegetable n
She only eats bread and **vegetables**.

le légume [luh lay•gewm] n
Elle ne se nourrit que de pain et de **légumes**.

Drinks

alcohol n
Too much **alcohol** is bad for your health.

l'alcool [lahl•kohl] m n
Boire trop **d'alcool** est mauvais pour la santé.

alcoholic adj
This restaurant does not serve **alcoholic** drinks.

alcoolisé, e [ahl•koh•lee•zay] adj
Ce restaurant ne sert pas de boissons **alcoolisées**.

also adv
Could I **also** have a glass of water, please?

aussi [oh•see] adv
Est-ce que je pourrais **aussi** avoir un verre d'eau, s'il vous plaît?

beer n
I'd like a **beer**, please.

la bière [lah bee•ehr] n
Je prendrai une **bière**, s'il vous plaît.

bottle n
We drank two **bottles** of wine with our meal last night.

la bouteille [lah boo•tehyuh] n
Nous avons bu deux **bouteilles** de vin avec notre repas, hier soir.

coffee n
Would you like a cup of **coffee** too?

le café [luh kah•fay] n
Prendrez-vous aussi un **café**?

drink n

I like soft **drinks**.
Would you like another **drink**?

la boisson; le verre
[lah bwah•sohN; luh vehr] n
J'aime **les boissons** sans alcool.
Prendrez-vous un autre **verre**?

to drink *v*
I'd like to sit in a pub and **drink** *beer.*

boire [bwar] *v*
J'aimerais m'installer dans un pub et **boire** *une bière.*

empty *adj*
My glass is **empty**. *Is there any more wine?*

vide [veed] *adj*
Mon verre est **vide**. *Est-ce qu'il reste du vin?*

hot chocolate *n*

In this café they make a very good **hot chocolate**.

le chocolat chaud
[luh choh•koh•lah shoh] *n*
Dans ce café ils font un très bon **chocolat chaud**.

juice *n*
Can I have some orange **juice**?

le jus [luh zhew] *n*
Puis-je avoir du **jus** *d'orange?*

milk *n*
Do you want **milk** *in your tea?*

le lait [luh leh] *n*
Voulez-vous du **lait** *dans votre thé?*

pint *n*
A **pint** *of beer, please.*

la pinte [lah pehNt] *n*
Une **pinte** *de bière, s'il vous plaît.*

tea *n*
Can I offer you a cup of **tea**?

le thé [luh tay] *n*
Puis-je vous offrir une tasse de **thé?**

to be thirsty *adj*
Are you **thirsty**? *Do you want a drink?*

avoir soif [ah•vwar swaf] *loc*
Avez-vous soif? *Voulez-vous boire quelque chose?*

water *n*
Can I have mineral **water**, *please?*

l'eau [loh] *n*
Puis-je avoir de **l'eau** *minérale, s'il vous plaît?*

wine *n*
Can I have a glass of white **wine** *with my lasagne, please?*

le vin [luh vehN] *n*
Puis-je avoir un verre de **vin** *blanc avec ma lasagne?*

always *adv*
You're **always** talking about food.

toujours [too·zhoor] *adv*
Tu parles **toujours** de manger.

and *conj*
Can I have an espresso **and** a glass of water, please?

et [ay] *conj*
Pourrais-je avoir un espresso **et** un verre d'eau, s'il vous plaît?

bill *n*
Can I have the **bill**, please?

la note [lah not] *n*
Apportez-moi **la note**, s'il vous plaît.

breakfast *n*

What time do you want **breakfast?**

le petit déjeuner
[luh puh·tee day·zhuh·nay] *n*
A quelle heure voulez-vous **le petit déjeuner?**

to have breakfast *loc*

Do you want **to have breakfast** together?

prendre le petit déjeuner
[praw·Ndruh luh puh·tee day·zhuh·nay] *loc*
Tu veux **prendre le petit déjeuner** ensemble?

to bring *v*
Could you **bring** us two coffees, please?

apporter [ah·por·tay] *v*
Pourriez-vous nous **apporter** deux cafés, s'il vous plaît?

but *conj*
The food here is expensive, **but** good.

mais [meh] *conj*
La nourriture ici est chère, **mais** bonne.

café *n*

Is there a **café** near here?

le café
[luh kah·fay] *n*
Est-ce qu'il y a un **café** dans le coin?

| **Cheers!** *interj* | **A votre santé! A la vôtre!**
[ah voh•truh sawN•tay!
ah lah voh•truh!] *loc* |
| *Cheers! To us!* | *À ta santé! À nous!* |

| **clean** *adj* | **propre** [pro•pruh] *adj* |
| *Are your hands **clean**?* | *Est-ce que tu as les mains **propres**?* |

| **cup** *n* | **la tasse** [lah tass] *n* |
| *Would you like a **cup** of coffee?* | *Voulez-vous une **tasse** de café?* |

| **to cut** *v* | **couper, découper**
[koo•pay, day•koo•pay] *v* |
| *Can you **cut** the cake?* | *Peux-tu **couper** le gâteau?* |

| **fork** *n* | **la fourchette** [lah foor•sheht] *n* |
| *Could I have a clean **fork**, please?* | *Pourrais-je avoir une **fourchette** propre?* |

| **glass** *n* | **le verre** [luh vehr] *n* |
| *A big **glass** of orange juice, please.* | *Un grand **verre** de jus d'orange, s'il vous plaît.* |

| **gram** *n Am*
gramme *n Brit.* | **le gramme** [luh gram]s |
| *There are 1000 **grams** in a kilogram.* | *Il y a 1000* [meel] ***grammes** dans un kilo.* |

Fact

1 gram **un gramme** = 1000 milligrams = 0.035 oz.
1 kilogram (kg) **un kilo(gramme)** = 1000 grams = 2.2 lb

kilo *n* **(kilogram** *n Am)* **(kilogramme** *n Brit.)* *I'd like two **kilos** of potatoes, please.*	**le kilo(gramme)** [luh kee•loh(gram)] *n* *Je voudrais 2 **kilos** de pommes de terre, s'il vous plaît.*
knife *n* *The **knives** and forks are on the table.*	**le couteau** [luh koo•toh] *n* *Les **couteaux** et les fourchettes sont sur la table.*
to have lunch *locution* *Do you want to **have lunch**?*	**déjeuner** [deh•zhuh•nay] *v* *Voulez-vous **déjeuner**?*
meal *n* *My brother often eats his **meals** in his room.*	**le repas** [luh ruh•pah] *n* *Mon frère prend souvent ses **repas** dans sa chambre.*
menu *n* *Could I have the **menu**, please?*	**le menu** [luh muh•new] *n* *Pourrais-je avoir **le menu?***
more *adv* *I must study **more**.*	**plus, davantage** [plewss, da•vawN•tazh] *adv* *Il faut que j'étudie **davantage**.*
one more *adj* *We need **one more** knife, please.*	**un autre, une autre** [uhN noh•truh, ew noh•truh] *n* *Il nous faut **un autre** couteau, s'il vous plaît.*
to open *v* *Shall we **open** a bottle?*	**Déboucher** [day•boo•shay] *v* *On **débouche** une bouteille?*
to pay *v* *Did you have **to pay** for the meal?*	**payer** [peh•yay] *v* *Est-ce que tu as dû **payer** ton repas?*

pepper *n*
Could I have the salt and **pepper,** please?

le poivre [luh pwah•vruh] *n*
Pourrais-je avoir le sel et **le poivre**?

plastic *n*
I don't like **plastic** forks.

le plastique [luh plas•teek] *n*
Je n'aime pas les fourchettes en **plastique**.

plate *n*
Could I have a different **plate** for the cheese?

l'assiette [lah•see•eht] *n*
Pourrais-je avoir une autre **assiette** pour le fromage?

restaurant *n*
We're going to the **restaurant** at about twelve.

le restaurant [luh rehs•toh•rawN] *n*
Nous allons au **restaurant** vers midi.

salt *n*
This soup needs more **salt**.

le sel [luh sehl] *n*
Cette soupe manque de **sel**.

saucer *n*
We need one more cup and **saucer**.

la soucoupe [lah soo•koop] *n*
Il nous faudrait une tasse et une **soucoupe** de plus.

to sit *v*

Sit down and be quiet!
A few days later I **sat** at their table.

s'asseoir; être assis, e [sa•swar; eh•trah•see, eh•trah•seez] *v*

Assieds-toi et tiens-toi tranquille!
Quelques jours plus tard, **j'étais assis** à leur table.

some more *adj*
We need **some more** water.

plus, encore [plewss, awN•kohr] *adv*
Il nous faut **plus** d'eau.

something *pron n sg*
Would you like **something** to drink?

quelque chose [kehl•kuh shoz] *pron*
Voulez-vous **quelque chose** à boire?

spoon *n*
*Waiter, could you bring me a clean **spoon**?*

la cuillère [lah kwee•yehr] *n*
*Garçon, pourriez-vous m'apporter une **cuillère** propre?*

sugar *n*
*Could I have the **sugar**, please?*

le sucre [luh sew•kruh] *n*
*Pourrais-je avoir **le sucre**?*

tip *n*
*Did you give the waiter a **tip**?*

le pourboire [luh poor•bwar] *n*
*Est-ce que tu as donné un **pourboire** au serveur?*

waiter *n*
waitress *n*
*We left the **waiter** a tip.*

le serveur [luh sehr•vuhr] *n*
la serveuse [la sehr•vuhz] *n*
*Nous avons laissé un pourboire au **serveur**.*

to want *v*
*Are you sure you don't **want** anything?*

vouloir [vool•wahr] *v*
*Tu es sûr que tu ne **veux** rien?*

will not, won't *v*
*Your dinner **won't** be ready before seven o'clock.*

*Votre repas ne **sera** pas prêt avant sept heures.*

Sports & Social

art *n*
*I don't like modern **art** very much.*

l'art [lahr] *n*
*Je n'aime pas beaucoup **l'art** moderne.*

ball *n*
*She bought a **ball** for her children to play with.*

le ballon [luh bah•lohN] *n*
*Elle a acheté un **ballon** pour que ses enfants jouent avec.*

because *conj*
We didn't go out for a walk **because** it was raining.

parce que [pahr•suh kuh] *conj*
Nous ne sommes pas sortis **parce qu'**il pleuvait.

before *prep*
He arrived **before** the party started.

avant [ah•vawN] *prep*
Il est arrivé **avant** le début de la fête.

boat *n*
There were a lot of **boats** on the lake.

le bateau [luh bah•toh] *n*
Il y avait de nombreux **bateaux** sur le lac.

book *n*
How many **books** did you buy in England?

le livre [luh lee•vruh] *n*
Combien de **livres** as-tu achetés en Angleterre?

to book *v*
I've **booked** a table for eight o'clock.

réserver [ray•zer•vay] *v*
J'ai **réservé** une table pour 20 [vehNt] heures.

camera *n*

It's okay. We can take the **camera.**

l'appareil photo [lah•pah•rehhy foh•toh] *n*
C'est d'accord, nous pouvons prendre **l'appareil photo**.

cannot, can't *v*

ne pas pouvoir; ne pas savoir [nuh pah poo•vwar; nuh pah sah•vwar] *loc*

I'm sorry but you **can't** swim here.

Désolé, mais vous **ne pouvez pas** nager ici.

I **cannot** play the violin.

Je **ne sais pas** jouer du violon.

cigarette *n*
Are you sure you don't want a **cigarette**?

la cigarette [lah see•gah•rehtt] *n*
Tu es sûr de ne pas vouloir une **cigarette**?

cinema *n Brit.*
movie theater *n Am.*
Do you want to go to the **cinema** with me?

le cinéma [luh see·nay·mah] *n*
Est-ce que tu veux venir au **cinéma** avec moi?

French speakers often use the abbreviation **le ciné** for the cinema.

---

to come *v*
I can **come** at three o'clock.

venir [vuh·neer] *v*
Je peux **venir** à quinze heures.

---

concert *n*
Are you going to the **concert** on Sunday?

le concert [luh kohN·sayr] *n*
Est-ce que tu vas au **concert** dimanche?

Congratulations! *interj*

Congratulations! You're the first.

Félicitations!
[fay·lee·see·tah·see·ohN!] *interj*
Félicitations! Vous êtes le premier.

---

end *n*
The **end** of the film was very interesting.

la fin [lah fehN] *n*
La fin du film était très intéressante.

---

film *n*
Where can I buy a new **film** for my camera?

la pellicule [lah pay·lee·kewl] *n*
Où puis-je acheter une **pellicule** pour mon appareil photo?

---

film *n Brit.*
movie *n Am.*
Jurassic Park was a great **movie**.

le film [luh film] *n*

Jurassic Park était un **film** génial.

football *n*

Where's the **football**?

le ballon de foot
[luh bah•lohN duh foot] *n*
Où est le **ballon de foot**?

Fact

French speakers often use the abbreviation **le foot** when talking about a game of football or a match.

---

fun *n*
We had a lot of **fun** at the party.

s'amuser [sah•mew•zay] *v*
Nous **nous sommes** beaucoup **amusés** à cette fête.

---

to go camping *loc*

We always **go camping** on holiday.

aller camper [ah•lay kawN•pay] *loc*
Nous allons toujours **camper** pendant les vacances.

---

to go for a walk *loc*

After dinner we went **for a walk**.

aller se promener [ah•lay suh proh•muh•nay] *loc*
Après le dîner, nous sommes **allés nous promener**.

---

to go hiking *loc*

Oregon is a great place to **go hiking**.

faire de la randonnée [fair duh lah rawN•doh•nay] *loc*
L'Oregon est une région idéale pour **faire de la randonnée**.

---

to go swimming *loc*
Do you want to **go swimming** this afternoon?

aller nager [ah•lay nah•zhay] *loc*
Ça te dirait **d'aller nager** cet après-midi?

golf *n*
We play **golf** at least twice a week.

le golf [luh golf] *n*
Nous jouons au **golf** au moins deux fois par semaine.

hobby *(pl hobbies)* *n*

John has got a lot of interesting **hobbies**.

le passe-temps, le hobby [luh pass•tawN, luh oh•bee] *n*
John a beaucoup de **passe-temps** intéressants.

in *prep*
There's live music every Sunday night **in** the pub.

au, à [oh, ah] *prep*
Il y a des concerts tous les dimanches soirs **au** pub.

Fact

The preposition **à** + **le** combine to **au** and **à** + **les** combine to **aux**.

invitation *n*

Thank you for the **invitation** to your party.

l'invitation [lehN•vee•tah•see•ohN] *n*
Merci pour **l'invitation** à votre soirée.

kind *n*
What **kind** of books does she like to read?

le genre [luh zhawN•ruh] *n*
Quel **genre** de livres aime-t-elle lire?

Let's ... *loc abbr let us*
Let's go out tonight!

Sortons ce soir!
[sohr•tohN suh swahr!]

to like *v*
I **like** driving.

aimer [ay•may] *v*
J'**aime** conduire.

to listen *v*
He's **listening** to his favorite music.

écouter [ay·koo·tay] *v*
Il **écoute** sa musique préférée.

---

music *n*
What kind of **music** does she like?

la musique [lah mew·zeek] *n*
Quel genre de **musique** aime-t-elle?

---

novel *n*
Have you read the latest **novel** by John Irving?

le roman [luh roh·mawN] *n*
As-tu lu le dernier **roman** de John Irving?

---

often *adv*
We **often** go to the cinema.

souvent [soo·vawN] *adv*
Nous allons **souvent** au cinéma.

---

other *adj*
Why don't you use the **other** camera?

autre [oh·truh] *adj*
Pourquoi tu ne te sers pas de l'**autre** appareil photo?

---

party *n*
We could have a **party** on Saturday.

la fête [lah feht] *n*
Nous pourrions organiser une **fête** samedi.

---

perhaps *adv*
Perhaps we could walk around the lake.

peut-être [puh teh·truh] *adv*
Peut-être pourrions-nous faire une promenade autour du lac.

---

photograph *n*

I've got a camera, so we can take a lot of **photographs**.

la photo(graphie) [lah foh·toh(grah·fee)] *n*
J'ai un appareil photo, alors nous pouvons prendre des **photos**.

---

plan *n*
What are your **plans** for tomorrow?

le projet [luh proh·zhay] *n*
Quels sont vos **projets** pour demain?

---

pub *n*
Can we meet in the **pub** around eight?

le pub [luh puhb] *n*
Pouvons-nous nous retrouver au **pub** vers 20 [vehNt] heures?

to read v
*Have you ever **read**
'Huckleberry Finn'?*

lire [leer] v
*As-tu **lu** "Les Aventures de
Huckleberry Finn"?*

---

sport n
Do you do much sport?

sport [luh spor] n
*Est-ce que tu fais beaucoup de **sport**?*

---

story n
*He told us the **story** about his
younger brother.*

l'histoire [lees·twar] n
*Il nous a raconté **l'histoire** de son
frère cadet.*

---

television n

*What's on **television** tonight?*

la télévision
[lah tay·lay·vee·zee·yohN] n
*Qu'est-ce qu'il y a à **la télévision**
ce soir?*

---

tennis n
*There's a **tennis** match on TV
this afternoon.*

le tennis [luh tay·niss] n
*Il y a un match de **tennis** ce soir à
a télé.*

---

ticket n

*I'm going to book four cinema
tickets. Okay?*

le billet (d'entrée)
[luh bee·yeh (dawN·tray)] n
*Je vais acheter quatre **billets** de
cinéma. D'accord?*

---

then adv
*First we went swimming and
then we had a tea in that new
café around the corner.*

puis [pwee] adv
*Pour commencer, nous sommes allés
nager, **puis** nous avons pris un
thé au nouveau café du coin.*

---

true adj
*It's a **true** story.*

vrai, e [vreh, vreh] adj
*C'est une histoire **vraie**.*

TV n
*What's on **TV** tonight?*

la télé [lah tay·lay] n
*Qu'est-ce qu'il y a à la **télé** ce soir?*

well *adv*	**bien** [bee•yehN] *adv*
She plays the piano very **well**.	Elle joue très **bien** du piano.
yet *adv*	**déjà; encore** [day•zhah; awN•kohr] *adv*
Have you seen him **yet**?	L'avez-vous **déjà** vu?
I haven't played tennis **yet** this summer.	Je n'ai pas **encore** joué au tennis cet été.

Shopping

bag *n*	**le sac** [luh sak] *n*
Please get the **bags**. They're in the car.	Va chercher **les sacs**, s'il te plaît. Ils sont restés dans la voiture.
to buy *v*	**acheter** [ash•tay] *v*
Where did you **buy** that shirt?	Où as-tu **acheté** cette chemise?
cash *n*	**les espèces** [leh zes•pess] *n*
Can I pay in **cash**?	Puis-je payer en **espèces?**
change *n*	**la monnaie** [lah moh•neh] *n*
Do you need **change** for the phone?	As-tu besoin de **monnaie** pour le téléphone?
Here's your receipt and **change**.	Voici votre reçu et votre **monnaie**.
cheap *adj*	**bon marché** [bohN mar•shay] *loc*
The hotel is **cheap**.	Cet hôtel est **bon marché**.

cheque *n Brit.* **check** *n Am.* *Can I pay by **check**?*	**le chèque** [luh shehk] *n* *Puis-je payer par **chèque**?*
to choose *v* *He wanted to **choose** a new one.*	**choisir** [shwa•zeer] *v* *Il voulait en **choisir** un autre.*
to close *v* *The supermarket **closes** at 10:00 p.m.*	**fermer** [fer•may] *v* *Le supermarché **ferme** à 22 heures.*
credit card *n* *Can you give me your **bank card** number?*	**la carte bancaire, la carte de crédit** [lah kart bawN•kehr, lah kart duh kray•dee] *n* *J'aurais besoin de votre numéro de **carte bancaire**.*
expensive *adj* *The new car was **expensive**.*	**cher, chère** [shehr, shehr] *adj* *La nouvelle voiture coûtait **cher**.*
to have ... as well *loc* *Do you **have** them in a size 39 **as well**?*	**avoir ... aussi** [ah•vwar ... oh•see] *loc* *Vous les **avez** en trente-neuf **aussi**?*
to help *v* *Can I **help** you?*	**aider** [ay•day] *v* *Puis-je vous **aider**?*
to lend *v* *Can you **lend** me some money?*	**prêter** [pray•tay] *v* *Peux-tu me **prêter** de l'argent?*
market *n* *There's a vegetable **market** in the centre of town.*	**le marché** [luh mar•shay] *n* *Il y a un **marché** de primeurs en centre-ville.*

money *n*
Have you got any **money** on you?

l'argent [lar•zhawN] *n*
As-tu de **l'argent** sur toi?

- - -

note *n*

Here's a five-pound **note**.

le billet (de banque)
[luh bee•yay (duh bawNk)] *n*
Voilà un **billet** de cinq livres.

- - -

open *adj*

Some of the big shops are **open** on Sundays.

ouvert, e [oo•vayr, oo•vayr•tuh] *adj*
Certains grands magasins sont **ouverts** le dimanche.

- - -

price *n*
It's the same **price** for the two of us.

le prix [luh pree] *n*
C'est le même **prix** pour nous deux.

- - -

to put ... down *v*
Why don't you **put** these heavy bags **down** for a moment?

poser [poh•zay] *v*
Pourquoi ne **poses**-tu pas ces grosses valises un instant?

- - -

receipt *n*
Could I have a **receipt**, please?

le reçu [luh ruh•sew] *n*
Pourrais-je avoir un **reçu**, s'il vous plaît?

- - -

to sell *v*
I **sold** my old bicycle on the Internet.

vendre [vawN•druh] *v*
J'ai **vendu** mon vieux vélo sur Internet.

- - -

shop *n Brit.*

store *n Am.*
I got this shirt at a little **shop** in the city.

le magasin, la boutique
[luh mah•gah•zehN, lah boo•teek] *n*

J'ai acheté cette chemise dans une petite **boutique** en ville.

shopping bag *n*	**le sac à provisions** [luh sak ah proh•vee•zee•ohN] *n*
*I put all the tomatoes in the **shopping bag**.*	*J'ai mis toutes les tomates dans **le sac à provisions**.*
size *n*	**la taille** [lah tahy] *n*
*She wants a small **size**.*	*Elle veut une petite **taille**.*
supermarket *n*	**le supermarché** [luh sew•pair•mar•shay] *n*
*I bought the wine in a **supermarket**.*	*J'ai acheté le vin dans un **supermarché**.*
tax *n*	**les impôts** [lay zehN•poh] *n*
*Are **taxes** high in your country?*	*Est-ce que **les impôts** sont élevés dans votre pays?*
very *adv*	**très** [treh] *adv*
*This watch was **very** expensive.*	*Cette montre a coûté **très** cher.*

Holidays & Travel

ago *adv*	**il y a** (when talking about time) [ee•lee•yah] *loc*
*I was in Amsterdam a month **ago**.*	*J'étais à Amsterdam **il y a** un mois.*
almost *adv*	**presque** [prehs•kuh] *adv*
*It's **almost** time to leave.*	*Il est **presque** l'heure de partir.*
area *n*	**la région** [lah ray•zhyohN] *n*
*There are so many beautiful places in the **area**.*	*Il y tellement de beaux endroits dans **la région**.*

to arrive *v*
*When do we **arrive** in London?*

arriver [ah·ree·vay] *v*
*Quand **arrivons-nous** à Londres?*

beach *n*

la plage [lah plahzh] *n*

to book *v*
*I **booked** a flight to Honolulu yesterday.*

réserver [ray·zer·vay] *v*
*J'ai **réservé** un billet d'avion pour Honolulu, hier.*

building *n*
*There are all kinds of interesting **buildings** in the area.*

le bâtiment [luh bah·tee·mawN] *n*
*Il y a de nombreux **bâtiments** intéressants dans ce quartier.*

to carry *v*
*Do we have to **carry** our luggage?*

porter [por·tay] *v*
*Devons-nous **porter** nos bagages?*

case *n*
*Can you carry my **case**?*

la valise [lah vah·leez] *n*
*Pouvez-vous porter ma **valise**?*

centre *n Brit.*
center *n Am.*
*I live in the **center** of town.*

le centre-ville
[luh sawN·truh·veel] *n*
*J'habite en **centre-ville**.*

to check in *v*
*We must **check in** at the airport at half past four.*

enregistrer [awN·ruh·zhees·tray] *v*
*Nous devons **enregistrer** à l'aéroport à 16h30.*

to check out *v*

*You have to **check out** by ten o'clock.*

libérer la chambre (d'hôtel)
[lee·bay·ray lah shawN·bruh (doh·tell)] *loc*
*Vous devez **libérer la chambre** avant 10 [deez] heures.*

church *n*
*Do you go to **church** on Sundays?*

l'église [lay·gleez] *n*
*Vas-tu à **l'église** le dimanche?*

city n	**la ville** [lah veel] n
Paris is a beautiful **city**, but London is nice too.	Paris est une belle **ville**, mais Londres l'est également.
corner n	**le coin de la rue** [luh kwehN duh lah rew] n
The new pub is on the **corner**.	Le nouveau pub se trouve au **coin de la rue**.
early adj	**tôt** [toh] adj
There is an **early** flight.	Il y a un vol **tôt** le matin.
early adv	**d'avance** [dah·vawNs] loc
The plane arrived ten minutes **early**.	Le vol est arrivé avec dix minutes **d'avance**.
to find v	**trouver** [troo·vay] v
Where can I **find** a supermarket?	Où puis-je **trouver** un supermarché?
to get back v	**revenir, rentrer** [ruh·vuh·neer, rawN·tray] v
When did you **get back**?	Quand êtes-vous **rentrés**?
group n	**le groupe** [luh groop] n
The **group** of children arrived on the eight o'clock train.	Le **groupe** d'enfants est arrivé par le train de 8 heures.
guest n	**l'invité, e** [lehN·vee·tay, lehN·vee·tay] n
Our **guests** get the best room.	Nous réservons à nos **invités** la meilleure chambre.
guide n	**le/la guide** [luh/lah geed] n
You can't visit this building without a **guide**.	Vous ne pouvez pas visiter ce bâtiment sans un **guide**.

guide book n	**le guide de voyage** [luh geed duh vwah•yazh] n
I bought a **guide book** for two dollars.	J'ai acheté un **guide de voyage** pour deux dollars.
heavy adj Your suitcase is very **heavy**.	**lourd, e** [loor, loord] adj Ta valise est très **lourde**.
hill n	**la colline, le coteau** [lah koh•leen, luh koh•toh] n
Go up the **hill**.	Allez en haut de **la colline**.
holiday n Brit. e.g. Holidays **vacation** n Am.	**les vacances** [lay vah•kawNs] n
Many Americans only have two weeks of **vacation** a year.	Beaucoup d'Américains n'ont que deux semaines de **vacances** par an.
hotel n Our **hotel** was about five kilometers out of town.	**l'hôtel** [loh•tell] n Notre **hôtel** se trouvait à environ cinq kilomètres de la ville.

Fact

L'hôtel de ville is larger than **la mairie**, which can also be found in a small village, but can be roughly translated as 'the town hall', and should not to be confused with **l'hôtel** (hotel). Formal occasions such as registry office weddings take place here.

information n sg	**les informations, les renseignements** [leh zehN•for•mah•see•ohN, leh rawN•seh•nee•uh•mawN] n

Have you got any **information** about the town?
Avez-vous des **renseignements** sur cette ville?

---

island n
It's a big **island**.
l'île [leel] n
C'est une grande **île**.

---

its pron neutre sg
I love Paris and **its** museums.
son, sa, ses [sohN, sah, seh] pron
J'aime Paris et **ses** musées.

---

lake n
Let's walk around the **lake** on Sunday evening.
le lac [luh lahk] n
Allons marcher autour du **lac** dimanche soir.

---

late adv
The plane arrived **late**.
en retard [awN ruh•tahr] loc
L'avion est arrivé **en retard**.

---

to look at v
Look at the sea over there!
regarder [ruh•gahr•day] v
Regarde la mer là-bas!

---

luggage n
Our **luggage** is too heavy.
les bagages [leh bah•gazh] n
Nos **bagages** sont trop lourds.

---

of prep
It's in the south **of** France.
de [duh] prep
C'est dans le sud **de** la France.

---

map n
la carte, le plan
[lah kart, luh plawN] n

You want to buy this **map**?
That's one pound and pence, twenty-five pence, please.
Voulez-vous acheter cette **carte**?
Cela fera une livre et vingt-cinq s'il vous plait.

---

mountain n
la montagne
[lah mohN•tahn•yuh] n

Mount Everest is the highest **mountain** in the world.
Le mont Everest est la plus haute **montagne** du monde.

park *n*
London has a lot of nice **parks**.

le parc [luh park] *n*
Londres a de très beaux **parcs**.

place *n*

This is the **place** where they found him.

l'endroit, le lieu
[lawN•drwah, luh lee•uh] *n*
Voici **l'endroit** où on l'a trouvé.

port *n*
I don't want to live near the **port**.

le port [luh pohr] *n*
Je n'ai pas envie de vivre près du **port**.

to push *v*
Look at the sign. You have to **push** the door.

pousser [poo•say] *v*
Regarde l'écriteau. Tu dois **pousser** la porte.

quiet *adj*

It's a nice, **quiet** village.

calme, tranquille
[kalm, trawN•keel] *adj*
Le village est joli et **tranquille**.

reception *n*

There's a letter for you at **reception**.

la réception
[lah ray•sehp•see•ohN] *n*
Une lettre vous attend à la **réception**.

river *n*
What's the name of that **river**?

la rivière [lah ree•vee•ehr] *n*
Quel est le nom de cette **rivière**?

sightseeing *n*
Sightseeing in Paris is really fun!

visiter [vee•zee•tay] *v*
Visiter Paris est un plaisir!

soon *adv*
They are coming **soon**.

bientôt [bee•ehN•toh] *adv*
Ils arrivent **bientôt**.

space *n*
Who was the first man in **space**?

l'espace [less•pass] *n*
Qui a été le premier homme dans **l'espace**?

to stay v	**rester; séjourner** [res·tay; say·zhoor·nay] v
*The ferry had to **stay** in port.*	*Le ferry a dû **rester** au port.*
*He is **staying** with friends.*	*Il **séjourne** chez des amis.*
to sunbathe v	**prendre un bain de soleil** [prawN·druh uhN behN duh soh·lehy] loc
*In summer I like to **sunbathe**.*	*En été j'aime **prendre des bains de soleil**.*
theatre n Brit. **theater** n Am.	**le théâtre** [luh tay·ah·truh] n
*The **theaters** are closed on Mondays.*	*Les **théâtres** sont fermés le lundi.*
there is (pl there are) loc	**il y a; il existe** [eel ee ah; eel eg·zist] loc
***There's** a new supermarket in town.*	***Il y a** un nouveau supermarché en ville.*
***There are** different kinds of chocolate.*	***Il existe** différentes sortes de chocolat.*
to think v	**penser, réfléchir; croire** [pawN·say, ray·flay·sheer; krwahr] v
*What do you **think** of the hotel?*	*Que **penses**-tu de l'hotel?*
*We were on the top floor, I **think**.*	*Nous étions au dernier étage, je **crois**.*
together adv	**ensemble** [awN·sawN·bluh] adv
*We went on holiday **together**.*	*Nous sommes partis en vacances **ensemble**.*
tour n	**la visite guidée** [lah vee·zeet gee·day] n

*How much are the sightseeing **tours**?*	*Combien coûtent **les visites guidées**?*
tourist *n* *There are millions of **tourists** in New York every year.*	**le/la touriste** [luh/lah too·rist] *n* *New York accueille des millions de **touristes** chaque année.*
town *n* *Oxford is not a very big **town**.*	**la ville** [lah veel] *n* *Oxford n'est pas une très grande **ville**.*
trip *n* *Have a nice **trip**!*	**le voyage** [luh vwa·yazh] *n* *Bon **voyage**!*
visit *n* ***Entry** is free for children.*	**la visite** [lah vee·zeet] *n* ***La visite** est gratuite pour les enfants.*
village *n* *It's a nice little **village**.*	**le village** [luh vee·lazh] *n* *C'est un joli petit **village**.*
to visit *v* *Last month we went to Cornwall to **visit** his parents.*	**rendre visite** [rawN·druh vee·zeet] *loc* *Le mois dernier, nous avons **rendu visite** à ses parents en Cornouailles.*
with *prep* *A room **with** or without a bath?*	**avec** [ah·vehk] *prep* *Voulez-vous une chambre **avec** ou sans salle de bains?*
without *prep* *A room with or **without** a bath?*	**sans** [sawN] *prep* *Voulez-vous une chambre avec ou **sans** salle de bains?*
world *n* *He thinks he's the best student in the **world**.*	**le monde** [luh mohNd] *n* *Il se prend pour le meilleur étudiant du **monde**.*

Essentials

Weather & Climate

again *adv*
It's raining **again** today.

de nouveau [duh noo·voh] *adv*
Il pleut **de nouveau** aujourd'hui.

air *n*
Let's get some fresh **air**.

l'air [lehr] *n*
Sortons prendre **l'air**.

cloudy *adj*
It was always **cloudy** in
the morning.

nuageux [new·ah·zhuh] *adj*
Le ciel était toujours **nuageux**
le matin.

cold *adj*
It's **cold** today. It was warmer
yesterday.

froid [frwah] *adj*
Il fait **froid** aujourd'hui. Il faisait
plus doux hier.

cool *adj*
It was very **cool** this morning.

frais [freh] *adj*
Il faisait très **frais** ce matin.

degree n
The temperature is
12 **degrees**.

le degré [luh duh•gray] n
La température est de 12 [dooz]
degrés.

---

dry adj
The weather is sunny and **dry**.

sec [sehk] adj
Le temps est ensoleillé et **sec**.

---

fine adj
The weather is **fine**.

beau [boh] adj
Il fait **beau**.

---

hot adj
It was too **hot** last summer.

chaud [shoh] adj
Il a fait trop **chaud** l'été dernier.

---

rain n
We had a lot of **rain** at
the weekend.

la pluie [lah plew•ee] n
Nous avons eu beaucoup de **pluie**
pendant le week-end.

---

to rain v
It **rained** all afternoon.

pleuvoir [pluh•vwar] v
Il a **plu** tout l'après-midi.

---

sunny adj

ensoleillé, e [awN•soh•leh•yay,
awN•soh•leh•yay] adj

Christmas Day was very **sunny**.

Le jour de Noël a été très **ensoleillé**.

---

temperature n

la température
[lah tawN•pay•rah•tewr] n

In central Australia the
temperatures can be very high.

Dans le centre de l'Australie, les
températures peuvent parfois
grimper très haut.

---

terrible adj

déplorable, affreux, euse
[day•ploh•ra•bluh, ah•fruh,
ah•fruhz] adj

The weather was **terrible**
last year.

Le temps a été **affreux** l'année
dernière.

---

warm adj	**chaud, e** [shoh, shohd] adj
It's **warm** in here.	Il fait **chaud** ici. Est-ce que je peux
Can I open window?	ouvrir la fenêtre?

| **weather** n | **le temps** [luh tawN] n |
| What beautiful **weather**! | Quel beau **temps**! |

wet adj	**humide; mouillé, e; trempé, e**
	[ew·meed; moo·yay, moo·yay;
	trawN·pay, trawN·pay] adj
Yesterday was very **wet**.	La journée d'hier a été très **humide**.
I forgot my umbrella and	J'ai oublié mon parapluie et me suis
got very **wet**.	retrouvé **trempé**.

wind n	**le vent** [luh vawN] n
There was a strong **wind**	**Le vent** a soufflé très fort la nuit
last night.	dernière.

windy adj	**venteux, de vent**
	[vawN·tuh, duh vawN] adj
We had a few **windy** days	Nous avons eu quelques jours **de**
in France.	**vent** en France.

Days of the Week

| **Monday** n | **le lundi** [luh luhN·dee] n |
| I don't like **Mondays**. | Je n'aime pas **le lundi**. |

| **Tuesday** n | **le mardi** [luh mar·dee] n |
| Last **Tuesday** I sold your books. | J'ai vendu tes livres **mardi** dernier. |

| **Wednesday** n | **le mercredi** |
| | [luh mehr·kruh·dee] n |

Wednesday is the day between Tuesday and Thursday.	*Le mercredi* suit le mardi et précède le jeudi.
Thursday n	**le jeudi** [luh zhuh•dee] n
I've got a date with Sylvie on **Thursday** night.	J'ai rendez-vous avec Sylvie **jeudi** soir.
Friday n	**le vendredi** [luh vawN•druh•dee] n
Thank God, it's **Friday**!	Dieu merci, on est **vendredi!**
Saturday n	**le samedi** [luh sam•dee] n
On **Saturdays** we go to the market in town.	*Le samedi* nous allons au marché en ville.
Sunday n	**le dimanche** [luh dee•mawNsh] n
I couldn't go to the party last **Sunday**. I was ill.	Je n'ai pas pu aller à la fête **dimanche** dernier. J'étais malade.
day n	**le jour, la journée** [luh zhoor, lah zhoor•nay] n
It was a very nice **day**.	C'était une très belle **journée**.
today adv	**aujourd'hui** [oh•zhoor•dwee] adv
What are you doing **today**?	Qu'est-ce que tu fais **aujourd'hui?**

Fact

La journée is used when you want to emphasize the course of the day. I'm going there during the day – **J'y vais pendant la journée** or 'What a day!' – **Quelle journée!**

yesterday adv
I saw him **yesterday** on the bus.

hier [ee·ehr] adv
Je l'ai croisé **hier** dans le bus.

tomorrow adv
I'm going to do it **tomorrow**.

demain [duh·mehN] adv
Je vais le faire **demain**.

week n
See you next **week**!

la semaine [lah suh·mehn] n
À **la semaine** prochaine!

weekend n
What are you doing this **weekend**?

le week-end [luh week·end] n
Qu'est-ce que tu fais ce **week-end**?

Special Days

bank holiday n Brit.
public holiday n Am.
The Fourth of July is a **public holiday** in the States.

jour férié [zhoor fay·ree·ay] n

Le 4 juillet est un **jour férié** aux Etats-Unis.

birthday n

The **birthday** party is next Friday.

l'anniversaire
[lah·nee·vehr·sehr] n
La fête **d'anniversaire** aura lieu vendredi prochain.

Christmas n
Are you going home for **Christmas**?

Noël [noh·ehll] n
Est-ce que tu rentres chez toi pour **Noël?**

Christmas Eve n

la veille de Noël
[vayhy duh noh·ehll] n

Christmas Day n

le jour de Noël
[zhoor duh noh·ehll] n

Fact

Réveillon is used for both Christmas Eve and New Year's Eve and refers in particular to the festive meal that is eaten on these occasions. See also p.121.

---

date *n*

What's the **date** today?
We had our first **date** on Christmas Eve four years ago.

la date; le rendez-vous (amoureux)
[lah datt; luh rawN•day•voo (ah•moo•ruh)] *n*
Quelle est **la date** d'aujourd'hui?
Notre premier **rendez-vous**, c'était la veille de Noël, il y a quatre ans.

---

to give *v*
He **gave** us a present at Christmas.

donner [doh•nay] *v*
Il nous a **donné** un cadeau à Noël.

Easter *n*
In many countries, **Easter** Monday is a holiday.

Pâques [pahk] *n*
Dans de nombreux pays, le lundi de **Pâques** est férié.

Merry Christmas! *loc*

Happy Christmas! *loc Brit.*
Happy Christmas to all of you!

Joyeux Noël!
[zhwa•yuh noh•ehll!] *loc*

Joyeux Noël à tous!

New Year's Eve *n*

New Year's Eve is the last day of the year.

la Saint-Sylvestre
[lah sehN seel•vehs•truh] *n*
La Saint-Sylvestre est le dernier jour de l'année.

New Year's Day n

New Year's Day is always on January the first.

le jour de l'An
[luh zhoor duh lawN] n
Le jour de l'An est toujours célébré le 1er janvier.

present n
Did you get a Christmas **present** from Terry too?

le cadeau [luh kah•doh] n
*Est-ce que tu as eu aussi un **cadeau** de Noël de la part de Terry?*

Months & Seasons

January n
January is the first month of the year.

janvier [zhawN•vee•ay] n
Janvier est le premier mois de l'année.

February n
In Germany **February** is the coldest month of the year.

février [fay•vree•ay] n
*En Allemagne, **février** est le mois le plus froid de l'année.*

March n
The weather in **March** is often cold and wet.

mars [mars] n
*En **mars**, le temps est souvent froid et humide.*

April n
My birthday is in **April**.

avril [ah•vreel] n
*Mon anniversaire tombe en **avril**.*

May n
I met him in **May**.

mai [meh] n
*Je l'ai rencontré en **mai**.*

June n
In **June** we always eat a lot of fruit and vegetables.

juin [jew•ehN] n
*En **juin** nous mangeons toujours beaucoup de fruits et de légumes.*

July n
Which American holiday is on the fourth of **July**?

juillet [jew•ee•yeh] n
Quelle fête américaine est célébrée le 4 [kah•truh] **juillet**?

August n
August is a winter month in Australia.

août [oot] n
Août est un mois d'hiver en Australie.

September n
Eva's birthday is on **September** the fourth.

septembre [sep•tawN•bruh] n
Eva fête son anniversaire le 4 **septembre**.

October n
The weather was nice in **October**.

octobre [ok•to•bruh] n
Il a fait beau en **octobre**.

November n
November is a beautiful month – in South Africa.

novembre [noh•vawN•bruh] n
Novembre est un mois magnifique – en Afrique du Sud.

December n
I was born on Christmas Day: **December** the twenty-fifth.

décembre [day•sawN•bruh] n
Je suis né le jour de Noël : le 25 **décembre**.

---

month n
We were in Melbourne a **month** ago.

le mois [luh mwah] n
Il y a un **mois**, nous étions à Melbourne.

Fact

The names of months are always used without the definite article except in dates. So for example, you might say **en juillet** (to refer to an event in July) but you would say **le quartorze juillet** (the 14th of July) to pinpoint an exact day in the month of July.

season *n*	**la saison** [lah seh·zohN] *n*
The four **seasons** are: spring, summer, autumn and winter.	Les quatre **saisons** sont : le printemps, l'été, l'automne et l'hiver.

autumn *n Brit.* **fall** *n Am.*	**l'automne** [loh·tohn] *n*
My birthday is in **autumn**.	Mon anniversaire tombe en **automne.**

spring *n*	**le printemps** [luh prehN·tawN] *n*
I met my wife in the **spring** of 1999.	J'ai rencontré ma femme au **printemps** 1999.

summer *n*	**l'été** [lay·tay] *n*
Why don't we go to Austria next **summer**?	Que dirais-tu d'aller en Autriche **l'été** prochain?

winter *n*	**l'hiver** [lee·vehr] *n*
Winter is the coldest season of the year.	**L'hiver** est la saison la plus froide de l'année.

year *n*	**l'année, l'an** [lah·nay, lawN] *n*
I saw the film perhaps ten **years** ago.	J'ai vu ce film il y a une dizaine **d'années** peut-être.

Fact

Ans is used to refer to someone's age – I'm 16 years old – **J'ai seize ans.** It is always used in the plural except when referring to one year olds – **Il a un an**. See also the New Year on page 123.

Time

afternoon n	**l'après-midi** [lah•preh•mee•dee] n
Can we meet in the **afternoon**?	Pouvons-nous nous voir cet **après-midi**?
a.m. also am	**du matin** [dew mah•tehN] n
The train leaves at eight **a.m.**	Le train part à 8 heures **du matin**.
at prep	**à** (heure) [ah] prep
The train arrives **at** six.	Le train arrive **à** 6 heures.
o'clock adv	**l'heure** [luhr] f n
It's 8 **o'clock**. Time for dinner.	Il est 20 heures, **l'heure** de dîner.

Fact

La soirée in French means the evening but it can also be used to mean a party or an evening reception.

around the clock loc	**24 heures sur 24** [vehNt•kah•truhr•sewr•vehNt•katr] loc
We must work **around the clock**.	Nous devons travailler **24 heures sur 24**.
evening n	**le soir, la soirée** [luh swar, lah swah•ray] n
Let's meet in the **evening**!	Retrouvons-nous ce **soir**!
hour n	**l'heure** [luhr] n
I needed a full **hour** to read the text.	Il m'a fallu une bonne **heure** pour lire le texte.

last *adj*	**dernier, ère** [dehr·nee·ay, dehr·nee·ehr] *adj*
What did you do **last** Monday?	Qu'est-ce que tu as fait lundi **dernier**?
midnight *n*	**minuit** [mee·nwee] *n*
She got home after **midnight**.	Elle est rentrée à la maison après **minuit**.
minute *n*	**la minute** [lah mee·newt] *n*
You need only twenty **minutes** by bus.	Le trajet en bus ne prend pas plus de vingt **minutes**.
morning *n*	**le matin** [luh mah·tehN] *n*
Take the earliest train in the **morning**!	Prenez le tout premier train **du matin**!
night *n*	**la nuit, le soir** [lah nwee, luh swar]
The **night** was cold and windy.	**La nuit** était froide et le vent soufflait.
What did you do last **night**?	Qu'est-ce que tu as fait hier **soir**?
now *adv*	**maintenant** [mehN·tuh·nawN] *adv*
She **now** lives in South Africa.	Elle vit en Afrique du Sud **maintenant**.
p.m. *also* pm	**de l'après-midi; du soir** [duh lah·preh·mee·dee; dew swar] *loc*
Our flight arrives at two **p.m.**	Notre vol arrive à 2 heures **de l'après-midi** / à 14 heures.
Our flight arrives at eight **p.m.**	Notre vol arrive à 8 heures **du soir** / à 20 heures.

second *n*	**la seconde** [lah suh·kohNd] *n*
*He arrived a few **seconds** later.*	*Il est arrivé quelques **secondes** plus tard.*
time *n*	**heure; temps** [uhr; tawN] *n*
*What's the **time**?* *I haven't got any **time**.*	*Quelle **heure** est-il?* *Je n'ai pas le **temps**.*
tonight *adv* *Would you like to go to a party with me **tonight**?*	**ce soir** [suh swar] *loc* *Que dirais-tu d'aller à une fête avec moi **ce soir**?*
watch *n*	**la montre** [lah mohN·truh] *n*
*What's the time? My **watch** has stopped.*	*Quelle heure est-il?* *Ma **montre** s'est arrêtée.*
What time ...? *loc*	**Quelle heure ...?** | [keh luhr ...?] *loc*
***What time** did you say?*	***Quelle heure** as-tu dit?*

Numbers

zero	**zéro** [zay·roh]
one	**un** [uhN]
first	**premier, ère** [pruh·mee·ay, pruh·mee·ehr]
two	**deux** [duh]

second	**deuxième** [duh·zee·ehm]
three	**trois** [trwah]
third	**troisième** [trwah·zee·ehm]
four	**quatre** [kah·truh]
fourth	**quatrième** [kah·tree·ehm]
five	**cinq** [sehNk]
fifth	**cinquième** [sehN·kee·ehm]
six	**six** [sees]
sixth	**sixième** [see·zee·ehm]
seven *n*	**sept** [seht]
seventh	**septième** [seh·tee·ehm]
eight	**huit** [weet]
eighth	**huitième** [wee·tee·ehm]
nine	**neuf** [nuhf]
ninth	**neuvième** [nuh·vee·ehm]
ten	**dix** [dees]
tenth	**dixième** [dee·zee·ehm]
eleven	**onze** [ohNz]
eleventh	**onzième** [ohN·zee·ehm]
twelve	**douze** [dooz]
twelfth	**douzième** [doo·zee·ehm]
thirteen	**treize** [trehz]

thirteenth	**treizième** [treh·zee·ehm]
fourteen	**quatorze** [kah·torz]
fourteenth	**quatorzième** [kah·tor·zee·ehm]
fifteen	**quinze** [kehNz]
fifteenth	**quinzième** [kehN·zee·ehm]
sixteen	**seize** [sehz]
sixteenth	**seizième** [seh·zee·ehm]
seventeen	**dix-sept** [dee·set]
seventeenth	**dix-septième** [dee·seh·tee·ehm]
eighteen	**dix-huit** [deez·weet]
eighteenth	**dix-huitième** [dee·zwee·tee·ehm]
nineteen	**dix-neuf** [deez·nuhf]
nineteenth	**dix-neuvième** [deez·nuh·vee·ehm]
twenty	**vingt** [vehN]
twentieth	**vingtième** [vehN·tee·ehm]
twenty-one	**vingt et un** [vehN·tay·uhN]
twenty-first	**vingt et unième** [vehN·tay·ew·nee·ehm]
twenty-two	**vingt-deux** [vehNt·duh]
twenty-second	**vingt-deuxième** [vehNt·duh·zee·ehm]
thirty	**trente** [trawNt]

thirtieth	**trentième** [trawN•tee•ehm]	
forty	**quarante** [kah•rawNt]	
fortieth	**quarantième** [kah•rawN•tee•ehm]	
fifty	**cinquante** [sehN•kawNt]	
fiftieth	**cinquantième** [sehN•kawN•tee•ehm]	
sixty	**soixante** [swa•sawNt]	
sixtieth	**soixantième** [swa•sawN•tee•ehm]	
seventy	**soixante-dix** [swah•sawNt•dees]	
seventieth	**soixante-dixième** [swah•sawNt•dee•zee•ehm]	
eighty	**quatre-vingt(s)** [kah•truh•vehN]	
eightieth	**quatre-vingtième** [kah•truh•vehN•tee•ehm]	
ninety	**quatre-vingt-dix** [kah•truh•vehN•dees]	
ninetieth	**quatre-vingt-dixième** [kah•truh•vehN•dee•zee•ehm]	
one hundred	**cent** [sawN]	
hundred	**cent** [sawN]	
hundredth	**centième** [sawN•tee•ehm]	
one thousand	**mille** [meel]	
thousand	**mille** [meel]	

thousandth	**millième** [mee·lee·ehm]
one million	**un million** [uhN mee·lee·ohN]
one billion	**un milliard** [uhN mee·lee·ahr]
to count v I **counted** ten parked cars.	**compter** [kohN·tay] J'ai **compté** dix voitures sur le parking.
number n He lives at house **number** two.	**le numéro** [luh new·may·roh] Il habite au **numéro** 2.

Quantities

all adj/pron **All** the students in the class are Irish. He gives her **all** his money.	**tout; tous, toutes** [too; too, toot] adj/pron **Tous** les élèves de la classe sont irlandais. Il lui donne **tout** son argent.
another adj Would you like **another** drink?	**un autre, une autre** [uhN noh·truh, ew noh·truh] adj Prendrez-vous un **autre** verre?
any adj Have you got **any** money? Have you got **any** information about these places?	 Avez-vous **de** l'argent? Avez-vous **des** informations sur ces endroits?
any adv He hasn't **any** information about this area.	**aucun, e** [oh·kuhN, oh·kewn] pron Il n'a **aucune** information sur cette région.

anything *pron*	quoi que ce soit; n'importe quoi [kwah kuh suh swah; nehN•pohr•tuh kwah] *loc*
Is there **anything** I can do for you? He would sell **anything**.	Y-a-t-il **quoi que ce soit** que je puisse faire pour vous? Il vendrait **n'importe quoi**.
both *adj* **Both** books are good.	les deux [leh duh] *loc* **Les deux** livres sont bons.
each *pron* **Each** of us pays fifty pounds a month.	chacun, e; chaque [shah•kuhN, shah•kewn; shak] *pron* **Chacun** de nous paie cinquante livres par mois.
enough *adj* There's not **enough** time.	assez, suffisamment [ah•say, sew•fee•zah•mawN] *adj* Il n'y a pas **assez** de temps.
every *adj* There's a disco **every** Sunday night in the pub.	chaque; tous les, toutes les [shak; too leh, toot leh] *adj* Le pub donne une soirée dansante **tous les** dimanches soirs.
everyone *pron sg* **Everyone** went home.	tout le monde [too luh mohNd] *loc* **Tout le monde** est rentré chez soi.
everything *pron sg* **Everything** was normal.	tout [too] *pron* **Tout** était normal.
extra *adj* I need the **extra** money.	supplémentaire [sew•play•mawN•tehr] *adj* J'ai besoin de cet argent **supplémentaire**.

few *adj* There were very **few** people there.	**quelques, peu** [kehl·kuh, puh] Il n'y avait que **quelques** personnes là-bas.
a few *adj* Give me **a few** minutes!	**quelques** [kehl·kuh] *adj* Donne-moi **quelques** minutes!
full *adj* The hotel is **full** this week.	**complet, ète** [kohN·play, kohN·pleht] *adj* L'hôtel est **complet** cette semaine.
half *n* I gave her the second **half**.	**la moitié** [lah mwah·tee·ay] *n* Je lui ai donné l'autre **moitié**.
half *adj* I bought **half** a kilo of beef.	**demi, e** [duh·mee, duh·mee] *adj* J'ai acheté un **demi**-kilo de bœuf.
a lot of *pron, abbr lots of* There are a **lot of** parks in the area.	**beaucoup de** [boh·koo duh] *loc* Il y a **beaucoup de** parcs dans les environs.
many *adj* Did you see **many** animals in Alaska? He has visited **many** countries.	**beaucoup de, de nombreux, un grand nombre de** [boh·koo duh, duh nohN·bruh, uhN grawN nohN·bruh duh] *loc* Avez-vous vu **beaucoup** d'animaux en Alaska? Il a visité **de nombreux** pays.

much *adj*
I don't want that **much** juice,
thank you.

très [treh] *adj*
Je n'ai pas **très** envie de jus de fruit,
merci.

no one *pron*
There's **no one** here at all!

personne [pehr·sohn] *pron*
Il n'y a absolument **personne**!

nobody *pron sg*
I went to the front door, but
there was **nobody** there.

personne [pehr·sohn] *pron*
Je suis allé ouvrir, mais il n'y avait
personne à la porte.

nothing *pron sg*
What are you doing? – **Nothing**.

rien [ree·ehN] *pron*
Qu'est-ce que tu fais? – **Rien**.

Fact

The preposition **de** + **le** combine to **du** and **de** + **les** combine to
des. Before a vowel (a,e,i,o,u) or a silent h **d'** is used. Similarly,
before a vowel (a,e,i,o,u) or a silent h the partitive article is **de l'**.

so *adv*

tellement, tant, autant
[teh·luh·mawN, tawN,
oh·tawN] *adv*

Why does he eat **so** much?

Pourquoi est-ce qu'il mange
autant?

some *adj*
There are **some** very interesting
people there.
Would you like **some** more tea?
I hope we can find **some** kind
of solution.

des, encore [deh, ehNkOhr] *art/adj*
Il y a **des** personnes très
intéressantes ici.
Voulez-vous **encore** du thé?
J'espère que nous parviendrons à
trouver **une** solution.

Asking Questions

answer n
*I got no **answer** from him.*

la réponse [lah ray•pohNs] n
*Je n'ai obtenu aucune **réponse** de lui.*

---

could v

Could you get tickets for the concert?

Could you tell me something about your country?

pouvoir (conditional) [poo•vwar] v

Pourriez-vous acheter des billets pour le concert?

Pourrais-tu me dire quelque chose à propos de ton pays?

how adv
How do I get to the station?

comment [koh•mawN] adv
Comment puis-je me rendre à la gare?

How about …? locution

How about something to eat?

Que diriez-vous…? [kuh dee•ree•ay voo] loc

Que diriez-vous de manger un morceau?

How are you doing? loc Am.

How are you doing? – I'm good. How about you?

Comment ça va? [koh•mawN sah vah?] loc

Comment ça va? – Bien, et toi?

How long ago… locution

How long ago was that?

il y a combien de temps [ee•lee•yah kohN•bee•yehN duh tawN] loc

C'était il y a combien de temps?

question *n*	**la question**
	[lah kehss•tee•yohN] *n*
*She asked him three **questions**.*	*Elle lui a posé trois **questions**.*

right *adj*	**bon, bonne; juste**
	[bohN, bonn; zhewst] *adj*
*Is this the **right** way to the market?*	*Est-ce que c'est la **bonne** direction pour le marché?*

| **shall** *v* | |
| ***Shall** I open the window?* | ***Voulez-vous** que j'ouvre la fenêtre?* |

| **to tell** *v* | **dire** [deer] *v* |
| *Can you **tell** me where we are?* | *Pouvez-vous me **dire** où nous sommes?* |

that *pron sg*	**ce (abbr of cela), cet, cette**
	[suh, set, set] *pron*
*What's **that**?*	*Qu'est-ce que **c**'est?*
*Who's **that** man?*	*Qui est **cet** homme?*

this *(pl these) pron sg*	**ce (abbr of cela), cet, cette**
	[suh, set, set] *pron*
*Is **this** his office?*	*Est-**ce** que c'est son bureau?*
*Do you like **this** car better?*	*Est-ce que tu préfères **cette** voiture?*
*Are **these** boots comfortable?*	***Ces** bottes sont-elles confortables?*

Fact

The pronoun **ça** is the colloquial abbreviation of **cela**. You will often hear this in the expression **ça va**? – how are you?

what *pron*	**qu'est-ce que; quoi**
	[kes•kuh; kwah] *pron*
What did you do last night?	*Qu'est-ce que tu as fait hier soir?*

What about …? *locution*	**Que diriez-vous …?**
	[kuh dee•ree•ay voo …?] *loc*
What about lunch in the pub around the corner?	*Que diriez-vous de déjeuner au pub du coin?*

What's the matter? *locution*	**Qu'est-ce qu'il y a?**
	[kess•keel ee ah?] *loc*
What's the matter with you?	*Qu'est-ce qu'il y a? Ça ne va pas?*

| **when** *adv* | **quand** [kawN] *adv* |
| *When do we arrive?* | *Quand arrivons-nous?* |

where *adv*	**où** [oo] *adv*
Where do you live?	*Où habites-tu?*
Where are you going, David?	*Où vas-tu, David?*

| **which** *adj* | **quel, quelle** [kehl, kehl] *adj* |
| *Which book do you want to read?* | *Quel livre veux-tu lire?* |

| **who** *pron* | **qui** [kee] *pron* |
| *Who told you that?* | *Qui t'a dit ça?* |

| **why** *adv* | **pourquoi** [poor•kwah] *adv* |
| *Why is she laughing?* | *Pourquoi rit-elle?* |

| **would** *v* | |
| *Would you mind passing me the salt?* | *Pourriez-vous me passer le sel?* |

Index

English

T

Y

Z